MAKE YOUR MARRIAGE
UNBREAKABLE

*Ten Steps to a Lifetime of Joy in an
Unbreakable, Divorce-Proof Marriage*

JIM KRUPKA

WESTBOW
PRESS®
A DIVISION OF THOMAS NELSON
& ZONDERVAN

WestBow Press books may be ordered through booksellers or by contacting:

WestBow Press
A Division of Thomas Nelson & Zondervan
1663 Liberty Drive
Bloomington, IN 47403
www.westbowpress.com
1 (866) 928-1240

ISBN: 978-1-9736-8259-2 (sc)
ISBN: 978-1-9736-8258-5 (e)

Print information available on the last page.

WestBow Press rev. date: 1/20/2020

Contents

Introduction

Sharing the Good News: You Can Have a Joy-Filled, Unbreakable Marriage

Congratulations! Since you're reading this, you're probably married, preparing to marry, or at least giving marriage some thought. In God's plan of creation, you are in a very good place. This book aims to share things that I have seen bring great joy to couples in marriage. It also draws from experience with couples who have suffered from painful marriages drawing from lessons learned from the things that kept them from realizing the joy of a good marriage. It is a great privilege to be with people as they prepare for a good marriage or work to make an existing marriage better. Through this, I am always learning something new that can help others and make my own marriage better.

This book draws from experiences with several hundred couples I have worked with on some aspect of marriage. Much of that work has been in a church setting. In using the word *church* in this book, I draw from my background in the Roman Catholic Church. However, my message is more generic than one faith tradition and applies across boundaries of any particular faith tradition.

What I have learned is offered in a personal way intended to be in the form of the kind of conversations I would have with you if you came to me wishing to marry or came seeking to make a struggling marriage work. Sadly, in many faith communities today, pastors do not have time to share the depth of experience and personal advice that comes from working with many marriages—good and bad. With several thousand families in a typical large urban church, the time for in-depth personal sharing is not there. That's why I offer the experiences and ideas in this book that come from years of marriage-building work. The keys to joy shared here are based on the joy that I continue to find in my own marriage as well as what I see in other couples on their personal paths toward joy in marriage.

I am a marriage optimist and advocate. Whether it is a first marriage or a subsequent marriage, more couples are coming prepared and ready to live a covenant marriage. Personally and as a minister, I have seen nothing in this world that gives more joy than a good marriage. The scripture writers agree. Throughout Old Testament faith history, images of marriage show up as the way God chooses to describe his love for humanity. The beautiful love poetry of Song of Songs, which is every bit as hot as a grocery store romance, gives us an image of God's love for his people. The writers can find no better image to describe God's love for human beings than the love of a man and woman in marriage.

Amid all the dismal pronouncements about low odds for marital success, there is good news. The odds of a lifelong marriage are better than popular media convey. First, the divorce rate in this country is declining and has been declining since the 1980s.[1] Divorce rates are lower for those married in the 1990s than for those married in the 1970s and 1980s. Couples married today are far less likely to divorce than their parents' generation who married in the 1970s. The higher incidence of divorce for older couples married in the 1970s gives an inaccurate picture of the likelihood that couples married today will divorce. Also skewing the divorce numbers are divorces after second or more marriages. Those married multiple times have a much higher divorce rate.[2] The statistics show the divorce rate for second marriages as 60 percent.[3] The dismal statistics not only make the overall divorce rate higher but also scare people who have been

[1] Belinda Luscombe, "How to Stay Married," *Special TIME Edition, The Science of Marriage.* 2017
[2] Bella DePaulo, PhD "What Is the Divorce Rate, Really?" *Psychology Today,* February 2, 2015, https://www.psychologytoday.com/us/blog/living-single/201702/what-is-the-divorce-rate-really
[3] Kalman Heller, PhD, *"The Myth of the High Rate of Divorce."* Psych Central, https://psychcentral.com/lib/the-myth-of-the-high-rate-of-divorce/

divorced away from building a new relationship and marriage. A failed first marriage sometimes leads to the assumption that the mess he or she made of marriage was so bad that the church would never allow them back to the altar again—for Eucharist or remarriage. From that assumption, the person simply marries outside the church, often in haste, and a second divorce happens without any of the help and support the church can give. That's how we end up with some of the very disturbing divorce rate numbers for subsequent marriages.

People, including church people, often throw out a statement that half of all marriages end in divorce. This is intended to shock those preparing for marriage. But for couples coming to the church today to marry, these figures are wrong. If we look at first marriages, the divorce rate was 40 percent around 1980 and dropped to 30 percent in the early 2000s.[4] Things that we encourage in the church, like taking time to prepare, significantly raise the odds. So does education. The divorce rate for college-educated women is now at or below 20 percent. By applying some of the things discussed in this book, the odds can be made even better. Instead of viewing marriage as a 50/50 shot at failure, let's look at it as a greater than 70 percent chance of lasting a lifetime. The numbers back this up. Couples married in the last twenty years are doing a better job of staying together than their parents' generation. Additionally, the couples who come to remarry in the church after divorce do a much better job than they did the first time or even their second or third at choosing a spouse. The church annulment process helps them understand what went wrong before and helps them avoid a repeat. That combined with formal preparation for a sacramental marriage greatly increases the likelihood of the new marriage lasting a lifetime.

Beyond that, there are things a couple can do to raise their odds of lifelong marriage to almost perfect. Couples that include actively praying together have an even higher likelihood of making it all the way through life in their first marriage. Such marriages succeed more than 70 percent of the time,

---

[4] Kalman Heller, PhD, "The Myth of the High Rate of Divorce." Psych Central, https://psychcentral.com/lib/the-myth-of-the-high-rate-of-divorce/The Myth of the High Rate of Divorce.

with some studies quoting a divorce rate of only 1 percent for those who pray together daily.[5] Finally, and this gets to a nearly rock solid guarantee of lifelong marriage, couples who practice natural family planning as part of living their faith have a 97 percent likelihood of staying married. I present this batch of statistics to point out the deeper you let God into your marriage, the more joy and certainty of lifelong marriage you will have.[6]

I am a cup-half-filled kind of guy. Among the couples I know who have married with any kind of preparation or witness from me over my years of ministry, I cannot think of one that ended in divorce. Some are now going on nearly twenty years. My observations don't square with the public rhetoric that marriage is a 50/50 deal. Even for second, third, or fourth marriages that I have had anything to do with, I cannot think of one that has ended in divorce. I am sure some have not made it, but they are in the minority. This has nothing to do with me but with people taking time to prepare for marriage and understanding what contributes to a healthy marriage and what does not, including faith and community in the marriage and maturity. They took the time to do the things that make a marriage unbreakable.

I take great joy in helping someone prepare for marriage. I believe in marriage as the avenue for tremendous joy in life. It is a wonderful gift from God designed to be the platform of society and our church. My joy is even greater when I can help someone coming to marry again after divorce. Some people spend years burdened by the thought that marriage in the church was impossible because of mistakes of the past. When a person realizes that the church is a compassionate home and that healing is possible, great things happen.

As you move forward, whether it is a first marriage or the chance to form a first sacramental, lifelong marriage after divorce, the words in this

---

[5] Dr. David Stoop, "The Couple That Prays Together," *Marriage and Family Matters* (Blog), *August 6, 2012*

[6] Richard J. Fehring, "The influence of contraception, abortion, and natural family planning on divorce rates as found in the 2006–2010 National Survey of Family Growth, *The Linacre Quarterly,* August 2015, https://www.ncbi.nlm.nih.gov/pmc/articles/PMC4536625/

book are to help you enjoy a deliberate and steady walk toward a joyful covenant marriage that lasts. Whatever your path has been, others have walked that path before. The lessons from experiences in those marriages are captured here to help you make your marriage even better. God has given us immense joy to be found as two become one. I want you to have that joy in abundance all the days of your life.

Part of my background is as a married Catholic clergyman—a permanent deacon. In this role, I have worked with people of diverse faiths and even non-faiths. The experiences and lessons in this book transcend the boundaries of any religious tradition. I come from the perspective of catholic with a small *c,* meaning "universal." There is much in the chapters that follow that will bring joy to a couple ready to live in a marriage that is unbreakable regardless of faith tradition.

Chapter 1

TALKING ABOUT MARRIAGE IS PERSONAL: WE ARE PLEASED TO MEET YOU

I prepared this book drawing from forty-six years as a husband and a father of five. Twenty of those years have been as a permanent deacon. In my life as a husband, I've experienced much of the real stuff of life in full partnership with my wife, Frances. There were parenting challenges, financial strains, job challenges, and unique to us, moving a dozen times in our first thirty years together. Frances was my first teacher on finding joy in marriage and has been the best of teachers. The messages here would not have depth and meaning without the experience of living the joy of marriage with Frances. While this book has one author, it has two inspirations. Many of the things shared in this book offer a window into our lives and what we have learned about marriage by living it. Again, we are pleased to meet you!

A little of our story sets the stage. We met on Thanksgiving Day 1972 at Fran's parents' ranch in western South Dakota. I was finishing engineering studies at South Dakota School of Mines. If you've ever been around a school of mines, especially in the late 1960s, you know that social life is desperately limited. In engineering schools in those days, there was a large absence of women. Most guys spent four years with a deeper relationship with their slide rule than with women. Most men graduated without ever having a date. My four years were not that extreme, but they were not far different from that.

1

JIM KRUPKA

I first saw Frances on the opposite side of our college basketball court in late 1971. I looked across and saw my classmate, John, with a pretty girl. My thoughts were shaped by experience. Hardly anyone got a date at that place, and guys in my circle were even less likely to get one. Beyond that, it was even less likely that that date would be pretty. The next Monday, I asked John, "Who was that pretty girl with you at the game?" He said in his South Dakota farmer voice, "Oh, that's my sister." In the normal pace of life on the prairie, it took John a year to introduce Frances to me. Actually, Fran's mother may have had more of a role in it than John. The following Thanksgiving, I was house-sitting with a friend for a professor. We were two lonely souls left in Rapid City for the holiday. Seemingly in compassion for our solitude, we were invited to the family ranch for Thanksgiving dinner. I did not have any special hint that there might be a romantic component to the invitation. But Fran got a hint from her mom. Frances's mother told her that John was bringing two friends for Thanksgiving dinner and, referring to me, said, "And he's Catholic!"

The dinner was fantastic from the perspective of a penny-pinching, dormitory-fed student. I took Frances's presence as nothing more than being there as part of the family. She was teaching math at a high school across the state. As a college student, I thought she was out of my league. Here she was a pretty, grown-up woman out on her own making big money as a teacher. She reminds me now how "not big" the money from that rural teaching job was.

That dinner led to a movie with her brothers, beginning a series of six long-distance dates over six months. Far sooner than I would advise, we decided to get married and did so the next Thanksgiving. After a simple wedding in Frances's home parish followed by a one-night hotel honeymoon, we spent our second married night in her childhood home. The next morning, we were on a plane back to Oklahoma City. My boss made it clear, "If you're not back by Monday noon, I can't pay you." We needed the money, and I got back to work by noon.

Since then, our lives have been an adventure that we could not have scripted. We have now been married forty-six years and are blessed with five grown children. We've had fourteen home addresses and experienced ordained life in the church for twenty years. Each day brings new challenges and adventures. We've discovered many things about each other, and much of that was learned working with couples looking to build joyful marriages of their own.

We began leading marriage preparation groups twenty years ago while living in London. We were transferred to the United Kingdom when the company I worked for was bought by a British company. Already ordained a deacon, I was granted the privilege of serving as a deacon in the city of London. Our large urban parish had a very diverse international population. The preparation groups usually included ten to fifteen couples. Most had long-term relationships and often were a mix of religions including nonreligious. We were invited to witness the marriage preparation weekend led by an Irish couple that was well established in the parish. Before the next year came around, the leadership baton was handed to us. When we moved back to the United States, we repeated the sequence. We were invited to help lead a session in our new hometown. By the next year, we had the lead. That sequence that moved us quickly from exposure to marriage preparation to commitment to lead says something about our passion for marriage and desire to share the joy of marriage. Having moved often, there were few core aspects of life that gave us continuity. The most basic was our marriage and immediate family that sprouted from it. The second was our church. These threads of continuity brought us to make marriage preparation core to our lives and ministry as a deacon couple.

Now forty-six years into our own journey of marriage, we know that we are much closer to the end of our marriage than the beginning. Life has taught us to know and appreciate the meaning of covenant in marriage. We know about romance as well as disillusionment. We know that with a covenant view of marriage, joy is there. As a deacon, I learn more every day about what it is to really live the covenant of marriage. In the church, we put the name "sacrament" on a marriage that is formed in the full covenant sense. As a deacon, I share celebrations of lifelong marriages most visible at things like weddings of adult children, golden anniversaries, and funerals. In those times, stories are shared that bring out the real deal of a joyful marriage that often go unnoticed. I also work with many people who formed marriages legally and ended in divorces and sadness. Some of these even started in church, with all the appearance of a sacrament. Often these marriages happened with a priest as witness and before a church full of people. Yet when they come to me, usually after a divorce, it is clear that the substance of a true covenant, the sacrament of marriage, never existed. For people in that spot, the church offers the annulment process. This process can offer healing by clarifying the absence of important dimensions of a sacramental commitment on their wedding day. I have seen no process with more integrity and compassion than the annulment petition process. The church delicately balances vigorous defense of marriage with compassion for people. In most cases after presenting evidence of lack of sacramental foundation, a decree of annulment or nullity is granted. In effect, this allows a person to move forward in life with the honest reality that they have never been in a sacramental marriage. They are now free to form a sacramental marriage for the first time. In the US, 88 percent of cases that are presented to marriage tribunals for formal consideration result in a decision. The other 12 percent are withdrawn or result in no decision. Of the 88 percent that end in a decision in which sentences are given, 96 percent of the decisions are in favor of nullity.[7] I do not take this as a symptom of easy annulment. I do take it, from my experience, that people who advance to the stage of making a formal annulment petition have benefited from significant pastoral counseling to get them to that stage. When they get to that stage, they have reflected enough on the truth of their circumstances to present a case with merit and integrity.

So what does this sad mention of divorce and annulment have to do with joy in marriage? The fact is that we can learn from human failings. Sometimes our own failings are our best teachers. For me, compassionately listening to others who have suffered from the absence of joy in marriage has been an amazing teacher. I can see the full-cycle effect of incomplete commitment to a covenant marriage and can see ways to help others avoid the same mistakes. Through my work assisting with annulment cases, I have gained much of what I share in this book as things that a man and woman can do to end up in a better spot and stay married. The aim is to end up with an unbreakable marriage with all the joy that comes with that.

---

[7] J. J. Ziegler, "Annulment Nation," *Catholic World Report,* https://www.catholicworldreport.com/2011/04/28/annulment-nation/, August 28, 2011

I have never met a couple who did not have the basic stuff to find joy in marriage, if they really want it. *Joy* is a word that is tossed around a lot in terms of pleasure. But marital joy is much deeper than mere pleasure. In my secular job, I have a coworker who has a standard wedding shower gift for couples. She gives couples—usually brides—two books: *Joy of Cooking*[8] and *Joy of Sex*.[9] Her message to brides is to pay attention to these two things, and you'll go a long way to having a smiling husband. As a man, I know that she is on to something, but there is so much more to finding the real joy of marriage. Helping you discover and nurture that joy is what this book is about.

---

[8] Irma S. Rombauer, *"The Joy of Cooking,"* Bobbs Merrill, Shribner, Indianapolis, Indiana, First published 1931

[9] Alex Comfort, *"The Joy of Sex,"* Crown Publishers, New York, 1972

Chapter 2

MARRIAGE: THE TREASURE GOD GAVE US THAT LIVES ON FROM THE PARADISE OF EDEN

There are two stories of creation in the Bible. The first is the one most people think of. That is the sequential steps of creation recorded in the first chapter of Genesis. This is the account Catholics hear during the Easter Vigil mass as the history of our faith is read.

> In the beginning, when God created the heavens and the earth—and the earth was without form or shape, with darkness over the abyss and a mighty wind sweeping over the waters—Then God said: Let there be light, and there was light. (Genesis 1:1–3)

The account moves from the gift of "light." Then there was formation of the oceans and land. Then came vegetation followed by distinctly the sun and the moon. Then Genesis 1:25 says, "Then God created the animals of all kinds." All of this took five of the six "working" days of creation. It is on day 6 that scripture says in Genesis 1:27, "God created mankind in his image; in the image of God he created them; male and female he created them." In this account, humanity is the last addition to the master plan of creation. As the sixth day ended, God proclaimed that all was "good" and rested on day 7.

This is the engineer's story of creation. All happens step by step in a logical way without much emotion.

The second story of creation is told in the second chapter of Genesis. In this account, humanity is the center of the creation story. Human beings are the focus around which the rest of creation happens. In Genesis 2:4–7, we read,

> This is the story of the heavens and the earth at their creation. When the LORD God made the earth and the heavens—there was no field shrub on earth and no grass of the field had sprouted, for the LORD God had sent no rain upon the earth and there was no man to till the ground, but a stream was welling up out of the earth and watering all the surface of the ground—then the LORD God formed the man out of the dust of the ground and blew into his nostrils the breath of life, and the man became a living being

Then in Genesis 2:8–9, we hear how the paradise was built around that human being.

> The LORD God planted a garden in Eden, in the east, and placed there the man whom he had formed. Out of the ground the LORD God made grow every tree that was delightful to look at and good for food, with the tree of life in the middle of the garden and the tree of the knowledge of good and evil.

Genesis 2:15 says, "The LORD God then took the man and settled him in the garden of Eden, to cultivate and care for it."

At this point, the scripture writer says, in Genesis 2:19–20,

> So the LORD God formed out of the ground all the wild animals and all the birds of the air, and he brought them to the man to see what he would call them; whatever the man called each living creature was then its name. The

man gave names to all the tame animals, all the birds of
the air, and all the wild animals.

We have the first human. Pope John Paul II, now St. John Paul II, describes the magnificence and completeness of that first human. He says, "This man is male and female."[10] Sometimes people like to humorously look at this story and hint that God did not quite get it right when he created Adam. These comments describe an unhappy Adam moping around Eden. That is not the case. The Pope used the term "Original Tranquility" to describe this peaceful state in the garden. Scripture conveys this image of tranquility by describing how Adam settled into the garden.

Next we read of God's idea that would bring creation to perfection. Genesis 2:18 says, "The LORD God said: It is not good for the man to be alone. I will make a helper suited to him."

At the conclusion of Genesis 2:20, then into verses 21 and 22, we begin the final path to the great gift of Eden.

But none proved to be a helper suited to the man. So the LORD God cast a deep sleep on the man, and while he was asleep, he took out one of his ribs and closed up its place with flesh. The LORD God then built the rib that he had taken from the man into a woman.

Take a moment to think about your wedding day. Even if you have been married for decades, think back to the first time you saw the person you married. Think of what it was like if you came chastely to that wedding night blessed and free to come together as man and wife for the first time. If you are preparing for marriage, think of how wonderful your wedding day will be if you save this treasure for that day. This is how Adam must have felt when he said in Genesis 2:23, "This one, at last, is bone of my bones and flesh of my flesh; This one shall be called 'woman,' for out of man this one has been taken."

---

[10] Pope John Paul II, "Meaning of Man's Original Solitude," General Audience in St. Peter's Square, October 10, 1979

Adam had already experienced his superiority to all the rest of creation. He alone had the ability to think and act to shape his destiny. He alone had an awareness of the divine. No other creature in the garden was like that. Now with Eve before him, Adam could see Eve was like him in being superior to all other creatures. But Adam could also see what we see on our wedding day: the differences that make us man and woman that complete each other.

At that point in Genesis 2:24, God explains how man and woman are to live together. God gives us the gift of marriage. God proclaims the goodness of what married men and women experience in their intimate life as they become one body. "That is why a man leaves his father and mother and clings to his wife, and the two of them become one body."

This second story of creation ends with the statement of peace and goodness that was present that day. Scripture (Genesis 2:25) simply says, "The man and his wife were both naked, yet they felt no shame."

When I am with a group preparing for marriage, I ask how many have heard of Original Sin. In most groups, all hands go up. Then I ask how many have heard of Original Innocence. Usually one or two at the most will raise a hand. St. John Paul II described the joy of man and wife coming to each other, recorded in Genesis as the state of Original Innocence.[11] I think this is a beautiful title. When we consider faith history as recorded in scripture, the first two chapters of Genesis, this second story of creation, this Original Innocence, is the only segment where there is total and perfect communion with God. Through those first two chapters, humanity has not made any election to have its own way over God's desires. There is no selfishness. There is no abuse of anything within creation. There is no exploitation of our existence as sexual beings. Man and woman are in complete harmony with God. In their "Original Innocence," Adam and Eve

- are naked without shame
- can see in their bodies the call to love

[11] Pope John Paul II, "Mystery of Man's Original Innocence," General Audience in St. Peter's Square, January 30, 1980

9

- were received by each other as a gift
- were affirmed by God as he saw that this joining of bodies was good
- feel deep peace and joy living the truth of their bodies in simplicity
- experience the reality of the communion of persons: "nuptial"

The Pope said, "In marriage … man and the woman express their willingness to become 'one flesh' and express in this sign the reciprocal gift of masculinity and femininity as the basis of the conjugal union of the persons."[12]

When we think of the goodness of God and ponder how important we are to him, it is valuable to remember this state of Original Innocence. It is also important to remember this beautiful condition of Original Innocence when we think of our own marriage. We have it just like Adam and Eve.

The history of our faith from Genesis 3 on is a constant state of God and humanity in a covenant where humanity is sometimes in harmony but often chooses its own way. Scripture records the ongoing relationship of God and humanity as full of transgressions away from the will of God. These transgressions are followed by God-given remedies as we work our way back to harmony with God. Through it all, God is true to his covenant. He does not abandon us. It is humanity that strays and needs to be brought back. In my Bible containing 1,539 pages, the Original Innocence section is four pages long. The rest of the Bible is life within the reality of Original Sin.

Quickly in the third chapter of Genesis, humanity chooses to do things according to selfish wishes, even though those first human beings were fully aware of God and his desires. That is the end of Original Innocence as humanity discovers shame. In Genesis 3:6–11 we read,

> The woman saw that the tree was good for food and
> pleasing to the eyes, and the tree was desirable for gaining
> wisdom. So she took some of its fruit and ate it; and she

---

[12] Pope John Paul II, "The Man-Person Becomes a Gift in the Freedom of Love," General Audience in St. Peter's Square, January 16, 1980

also gave some to her husband, who was with her, and he ate it. Then the eyes of both of them were opened, and they knew that they were naked; so they sewed fig leaves together and made loincloths for themselves. When they heard the sound of the LORD God walking about in the garden at the breezy time of the day the man and his wife hid themselves from the LORD God among the trees of the garden. The LORD God then called to the man and asked him: Where are you? He answered, "I heard you in the garden; but I was afraid, because I was naked, so I hid." Then God asked: Who told you that you were naked? Have you eaten from the tree of which I had forbidden you to eat?

This passage conveys an important thing about our sexuality and shame. It is not being naked with uncovered skin that brings us real shame. It is the things that we do that we do not want anyone to see that give us shame and make us want to hide. Think about shame in the context of our sexual existence and how it exists when we cross a boundary of covenant level unity with the will of God and move into some space driven by our own selfishness.

- Shame is an indication of sin.
- Shame is a symptom of detachment from love.
- Only nakedness that makes woman an object for man or man an object for woman is a source of shame.
- Shame takes the place of absolute trust.

In a world filled with sexual exploitation of all kinds, marriage is one place where the human body and our differences as men and women are glorious and a treasure. It is in marriage that we can still find a bit of Eden and be in all ways naked without shame.

Challenges to Joy: Fruits of the Fall

The fall of humanity in the Garden of Eden established the reality that we humans like to have things our own way. We can be selfish in a way that opposes self-giving love. Our eyes were opened to choose between what we know is right and what is purely self-serving pleasure. In Genesis 3:22, we read, "Then the LORD God said: See! The man has become like one of us, knowing good and evil!"

The words tell it like it is. We retained the ability—the power of intellect—that sets us above all other creatures. With that intellect and the experience we can choose for our own pleasure, we can perceive options. We can be tempted emotionally to act in ways that we know are not what God is calling us to do.

Pope John Paul II addressed life in this world where we can still enjoy the gifts of Original Innocence through our humanity, our sexuality within marriage. He also described the reality of life complete with temptations and social pressures that emanate from our own sensual urges. In a series of 129 talks in the late 1970s and early 1980s, he talked about the gift and purpose of human existence.[13] He talked about the role of our human bodies in God's plan. He summarized Church teaching and tradition about love and sexuality in God's plan all set in a modern context. The talks are publicly available and worth reading on their own. The series has taken on the identity as Theology of the Body.

The ideas presented in Theology of the Body rest on the following important truths:

- Human beings were created in the image of God.
- Men and women cannot live without love.
- The body is a good and important part of human existence.
- Man and woman from the beginning form a communion of persons that is an expression of God's communion with humanity.

---

[13] Pope John Paul II, *L'Osservatore Romano* Weekly Edition in English, 10 September 1979 to 3 December 1984

In his teaching, the pope addressed the following threats to this good and divine plan:

- lust
- uncontrolled desire
- adultery
- lack of openness to fertility

When we look at the world around us, it is easy to see each of these threats alive and well. The problem is that giving in to uncontrolled desire and lust draws us away from any path to satisfaction. If you know some people who are promiscuous sexually, do they ever get enough? It seems the more they stray, adding partner after partner, the less satisfied they are. They always need more. We read about this in the book of Sirach. "For burning passion is a blazing fire, not to be quenched till it burns itself out: A man given to sins of the flesh, who never stops until the fire breaks forth" (Sirach 23:16).

What happens is that lust redirects sexual desire from its presence in Original Innocence to pure pleasure. No longer are man and woman gifts to each other; they are objects of desire for pleasure. Taken to its extreme, lust makes the purpose of the object, the other human being, fulfillment of sexual need and nothing else. Gone is dignity, gone is openness to creation of life, and gone is real communion of persons. Lust can never satisfy. Succumbing to lust leads to destruction.

In Matthew 5:27–28, Jesus refocused humanity back to creation.

> You have heard that it was said, "You shall not commit adultery." But I say to you, everyone who looks at a woman with lust has already committed adultery with her in his heart.

Here Jesus is not talking about the emotions we get when we see a beautiful woman or handsome man at the beach. He is talking about letting that emotion of appreciation of beauty move to desire and imaginations about how to possess that other person. What Jesus is doing is turning the issue of adultery inward to the heart. That is where the sin begins, even if we do not actually act to fulfill our desires. A man or woman may not act on their desires because of fear of consequences in society, but their emotional action on desire draws them away from a truly loving bond with their spouse.

St. John Paul II took the courageous step of saying that adultery of the heart can even happen toward one's spouse. He is saying that when the heart is undisciplined, the nuptial bond of love is broken. When the line is crossed from self-giving to selfish, the spouse becomes just a possession and target for personal enjoyment. In a crude sense, the person becomes merely an object for relief. Even lack of openness to fertility erodes the dignity of the human act of sexual love from full self-giving to pleasure and use without responsible love.

Taken in total, the Pope did not downplay the excitement associated with physical intimacy. In his words, we can feel his background as an actor and playwright. He says,

> Love unleashes a special experience of the beautiful, which focuses on what is visible, but at the same time involves the entire person. The experience of beauty gives rise to satisfaction, which is mutual.[14]

To wrap up this section on the gift of marriage and joy as sexual beings, we need to celebrate the continuation of Original Innocence in our married lives. We also need to recognize our weakness and vulnerability to risks and threats to joy. We need to be continuously aware of when we are moving toward that line between self-giving and selfish. There will be times in marriage when we will be drawn toward that line. Awareness at those times can be a powerful tool to pull us away from the edge before we fall.

When you feel the mental distractions that come with lust and desire, think of how much your spouse means to you. Mentally focus on things that bring joy to your marriage rather than just pleasure for you. A mental

---

[14] Pope John Paul II, "Return to the Subject of Divine Human Love in the Divine Plan," General Audience in St. Peter's Square, May 23, 1984

exercise that helps is simply to think of all the love that has transpired between the two of you since you first came together. Suddenly, you will appreciate more what you have. Think about how you found and continue to find exciting joy in your marriage that is so much better than whatever crept into your head trying to lure you away from your marriage. Spend time meditating and imagining ways to experience that excitement in a way that builds joy in your marriage. I will present more on how to do this later in sections on communication and sex, but for now, celebrate this gift from God. What a treasure we have as women and men being able to live out this gift!

Chapter 3

FINDING THE JOY OF AN UNBREAKABLE MARRIAGE: THE COVENANT ADVANTAGE

Frances and I start our group marriage preparation sessions with an icebreaker. We ask each person to say a few things about themselves. We ask them to share things like how they met, what they do, and where they plan to marry. We also ask them to describe one romantic thing their fiancé has done for them. The stories are amazing. We hear about love at first sight as well as relationships that have been brewing for decades. Everybody's story is different.

For Frances and me, with only six dates in six months before deciding to marry, it was more love at first sight. That felt wonderful, but in many ways, we were not prepared for marriage. We were so locked in the romance phase of our relationship that we did not see many things that would have been good to know about each other. By our wedding day, we knew little about the basic personality wiring of each other. What we know now tells us that we are not the greatest match when it comes to personality drivers and things that make it emotionally easy for a man and woman to live together. What has kept us together long enough to discover the immense joy that comes from a lasting marriage is our covenant commitment. We both knew going into our wedding day that saying, "I do," to each other was unbreakable. Neither of us imagined any circumstance that would lead to divorce. That simple commitment allowed us to play and pray through times where those challenges would otherwise have broken us as a couple. In my work as a deacon, I have seen couples recover from all kinds of hurts and marital disasters. I've also seen couples split over things that could be fixed. The core difference is commitment and willingness to live a covenant-type relationship.

By covenant relationship, we can look first to our faith history as a model. The Bible records the long back and forth relationship between God and humanity expressed in the Old Testament. The Hebrew scriptures describe a long history of good times and bad lived within an enduring and unbreakable covenant. In faith history, the moral of the story is humanity, as one party to the covenant, cannot quit on God. Even within our free will, there really is no option that gives any life. As far as the other party, God, we have seen since creation that he does not quit on us. That is what happens in a covenant. This is the model for marriage. In fact, as we read scripture, the covenant of marriage and God's covenant with humankind are used back and forth as examples to teach about the other. In the exciting poetry of Song of Songs, the scripture writer uses the romantic relationship between a man and woman as a model for God's love for us. In Hosea, a less than perfect marriage is given as the model for God's unfailing commitment to us, even when we are unfaithful. The writers can find no better way to teach us about the immense and glorious love of God for humanity than the love of husband and wife. Going the other way, the church is depicted as the bride of Christ. The writers can find no better way to talk about the loving and intimate communion of God for his church than marriage.

So as a foundation for a sustainable path to joy in marriage, we need to understand the difference between forming a marriage with a covenant commitment and all the other ways a marriage can be formed. Think about the creation story. After man and woman were created in the bliss of paradise, God asked Adam and Eve to respect him by giving to God what was his. In the simplest sense, this meant respect and obedience described in terms of "Don't eat the apple." In my faith tradition as a Catholic, I respect the stories in the Bible as primarily giving us a moral lesson. The purpose of scripture is not to be a literal history book. Whether this initial covenant with God involved an apple or other form of respect is not important. What is important is the basic moral lesson. That lesson is that God gave humanity everything. He wanted respect that comes from humanity choosing for him rather than yielding to our own urges. However, in the Adam and Eve story, human urges prevail. As that apple is eaten, suddenly there is awareness that something is wrong. Humanity discovers shame. Our first ancestors knew that they had failed on their obligations under the covenant. In view of this violation of what God expected from humanity, what does he do? He banishes Adam and Eve from the garden and brings on the trials of work and childbirth. But God did not abandon humanity. The covenant continued unbroken. Remedies had to happen, and we humans, as the straying partner, had to mend our ways, but God continued his relationship with us. That is a key part of a covenant. It is unbreakable until it is completed. If two parties really are in a covenant relationship, the relationship continues even on the worst of days. Remedies are found, and joy returns.

In the secular world, there are many ways to form a marriage that stand the scrutiny of law but are not a true covenant. Marriages happen on beaches and hilltops. They happen in front of magistrates and ship captains. They happen with and without prayer. Importantly, they sometimes happen with conditions. The conditions may be formal as in a prenuptial agreement that openly recognizes the possibility of divorce. More often, the conditions are not on paper or even verbalized. One or both parties may come to the wedding ready to love and be faithful to the other as long as the marriage continues to meet some picture of marriage in his or her mind. They may come with an understanding that if some failing occurs, often infidelity, the marriage is ended. That is not a covenant foundation. That is better termed a contract.

It is easy to see the difference between a contract and a covenant. Looking at secular law, a covenant is an agreement between two or more persons to do or not do something. It is a solemn promise. Often that promise is made binding by a seal. For example, covenants that come with a neighborhood describe the basic terms of agreement between the neighborhood and homeowners. These covenant terms are superior to any contractual arrangement a homeowner might have for a specific service. A legal covenant is enduring and does not have an end except at complete fulfilment. A covenant requires that the parties be competent to enter the covenant. For example, an infant or impaired person cannot properly form a covenant. Breaches of covenant require remedies designed to bring erring parties back to compliance.

Marriage covenants and God's basic covenants with humanity are similar. They are solemn and formed with sacred and physical seals that are visible during the rite of marriage and private in the physical consummation of the marriage. The man and woman must be of the maturity, knowledge, and free will to form the marriage. There is no end until complete fulfilment at the death of one of the parties. There may be times when one party or the other strays from the full intent of the covenant and remedies are proper. Remedies would be things like counselling or even temporary separations. But through it all, the covenant endures.

Different from a covenant, a contract serves some specific purpose as an agreement between parties. A contract is for a period of time and has an end. A contract provides terms that spell out when a party is in default usually accompanied by dissolution terms. If one or the other is not performing up to the contract, it ends. Penalties are paid, and it is done. With that end, parties are free to contract for a similar service with someone else. Some people act like that is proper for marriage. Increasingly people talk about serial marriage where two people stay together long enough to complete a phase of life, such as raising a child. When that task is done, both can move on to new partners for the next phase of life. The argument is that life is so much longer than it was at the beginning of time. They reason that marriage in the lifelong sense does not make sense when our lives are so long. This is set up with a prenuptial agreement that is based on the possibility of a divorce.

Imagine how empty life would be if God's relationship with us were a simple contract rather than an enduring covenant. Likewise imagine what humanity would be like if marriage were merely a contractual arrangement rather than a covenant. If we ever needed covenant, lifelong marriage, we need it now when we are living longer. As more of us get into the empty nest stage of life, we will realize the need for the joy that comes from a good marriage. Next time you are at a wedding, look at the couples who have been together for forty or fifty years. See what they have and how rich they are compared to those who through their own action have had a few marital restarts with new partners.

Your wedding day sealed or will seal a covenant of love between you and your bride or groom. The two of you make the covenant. In the church, we call formation of that covenant of marriage a sacrament. Like other sacraments, marriage is not magic. The mere fact that a minister listens to a man and woman say yes to the questions is not enough. In fact, the real ministers of the sacrament of marriage are the man and woman. The priest, deacon, or other minister are witnesses. For a marriage to be truly sacramental, it takes a covenant commitment without reservation from the woman and man. The church is there to witness and support the sacrament of marriage, not make the sacrament.

As a minister in the church, I take preparation of couples for marriage as one of the most sacred duties I perform. The time and effort my wife and I put into preparing people for marriage is the church's gift and duty. But as ministers in the church, we can only do so much. There are times during the preparation process when it is evident that something is lacking in a couple's readiness to enter a covenant marriage. That is balanced by our recognition that we have no way of knowing what is really in the hearts and heads of the man and woman wanting to be married. Mature and faithful men and women have a right to marry. It is at those times that as a minister I offer the strongest advice I can by encouraging counselling, encouraging a couple to take more time, or otherwise discerning whether they are ready to form the covenant. In effect, what I am doing is looking ahead to avoid the future need of sad and difficult remedies when the marriage hits problems down the road. The bottom line is that the minister in the church cannot form the covenant. The man and woman are the ministers of the sacrament of marriage.

I got a confirmation class question one time from a high school student. "If Janie and I are stranded on a deserted island and never see a priest again, could we have a sacramental marriage?" On thinking about it, in that extreme, the answer would have to be yes. If those two are fully committed to a lifetime of fidelity, open to life, and come to seek marriage freely with God as a witness and partner, they are forming a covenant. They are reliving the marriage in Eden. They are being full and true to the essence of the sacrament. On the other hand, there are couples who, after receiving all that the church can offer in the form of caution and preparation, still seem to lack the basics to form a true sacramental commitment. They are adamant in wanting to move forward with marriage. If they have done all that the church asked in preparation, on consultation with the pastor, the wedding happens. When I experience this, the fear I have is that someone five or ten years out will be dealing with them after divorce. I always pray that I am wrong. My wish and prayer are that at their fiftieth anniversary they will joke about all the cautions the deacon gave them about going ahead and how wrong he was. But from my experience working with divorced people seeking annulments, I know that the presence of a priest and church full of people is not enough to form a sacrament when the man and woman are not ready. To really get on the road to joy in marriage, take the time to be ready and take advantage of all the help the church has for you.

Like so many other factors that affect joy in marriage, if you are already married, maybe you did not have the time to really be ready. It is not too late to fill the gaps. Whether you are married for a few years or decades, renew your covenant level commitment in your marriage. The benefit you have is time together. Years of marriage have given you the chance to experience the full cycle that lies beyond the initial blinding bliss of romance. At some time or another, all of us have that romantic bubble broken. That disillusionment after romance is crushing. But getting through that valley is the path to joy. As you grow in marriage, you will become fully aware of your walk as a couple through that disillusionment valley. This awareness can give you an incredible advantage in reaching boundless joy in marriage. When you renew your covenant commitment to each other, you will have an incredible advantage over those who continue to be united in a contract way. With your covenant advantage, you can work through any rough patch. Those living with the possibility of an "out" under a spoken or unspoken contact out will fail. In your covenant marriage, you will find joy that they will never know.

The Covenant Questions on Your Wedding Day: Foundation, Commitment, and Signs

On your wedding day, before your vows, you will be or were asked three questions. In the Catholic marriage rite, they are called "the questions before the consent." These three questions are core to forming the covenant of marriage. They establish that both man and woman are coming freely and are able to form a valid covenant. They establish that both are truly ready to commit to the core elements of marriage: unity and openness to life. Focus on these questions is an important part of our marriage preparation helping couples really be ready to commit to each other on their wedding day. I put so much focus on these questions because these are also the three areas that I see most often when I help someone prepare an annulment petition after divorce. After divorce, there is often strong evidence that one or both parties in the failed marriage lacked real commitment on the couple's wedding day.

The questions are basic and simple. In the new Rite of Marriage,[15] the questions are as follow:

> Celebrant: [Name] and [name], have you come here to enter into marriage without coercion, freely and wholeheartedly?

> The bridegroom and bride: I have.

---

[15] United States Conference of Catholic Bishops, "The Order of Celebrating Matrimony," Catholic Book Publishing Company, 2016

Celebrant: Are you prepared, as you follow the path of marriage, to love and honor each other for as long as you both shall live?

The bridegroom and bride: I am.

Celebrant: Are you prepared to accept children lovingly from God and to bring them up according to the law of Christ and his church?

The bridegroom and bride: I am.

Every couple knows what to say as the "right" answer in front of a church full of people. But saying the words and actually committing to live them are two different things. There are many things that can get in the way of making a covenant.

The Path Toward Honest Answers to the Covenant-Building Questions

1. Have you come here to enter into marriage without coercion, freely and wholeheartedly?

Forced marriage is not generally a factor in Western society. However, there are many things that in modern society inhibit a person's ability to be fully free on their wedding day. A point to consider before saying yes to the question is "Are you fully able to say no on that day?" With many couples cohabitating before their wedding day, this is a big issue. Many come to the altar already sharing a mortgage, civil commitments, and sometimes the responsibilities of a child. If these factors already bind a man and woman together, there is not a free choice available on that wedding day. Lack of a fully free choice to marry can also come from social or family pressure. It can come from economic pressure or need to escape some other circumstance like loneliness. This is why the church requires preparation time and encourages couples not to live together before marriage. During this time, couples have time and can get help addressing the factors that inhibit a truly free will choice to marry.

Entering a marriage under some form of pressure is not a recipe for long-term joy. There will always be an element of "I had to do this" in the life of the couple. That emotion is impossible to hide from your spouse or yourself. When hard times hit, trying to save a marriage that was a compromise to begin with is hard.

In our society, this first question seems a little silly. But it is extremely important as the most fundamental question in making a covenant. A person must be a participant by choice without reservation. If you feel any reservation, take some extra time and get some counselling. Fortunately, most people know in their hearts that their chosen is right for them. They don't need to play mental games making a logical case for their choice. In that case, the first covenant question on the wedding day is an easy one.

If you are married and remember some factors that brought pressure on you to marry, there is still room to find that path of covenant love and joy. I am reminded of a conversation with a missionary priest from India. My wife and I were having dinner with him the weekend I was invited to his parish to give a promotion talk on behalf of the Maryknoll Missions. Somehow during dinner, we talked about marriage preparation. The priest told us how much more enduring marriages are in his rural part of India. He told us that marriages are arranged. My first thought was *How sad*. But as he talked, the idea gained more traction. He described the matchmaking process in his homeland as one where the families of the young woman and man become aware of a potential match. Before the young people can "date," a large group from one family visits the other family. They establish a chemistry of affirmation for what might develop before the couple can dive into the romance pond. If both families are happy with the match, the couple can move quickly toward marriage. The priest said that the couple may not be head over heels in romantic love like Western brides and grooms. But with the deep support of families, they grow in love as a result of working through the tough, postromance things that happen in life. They really gain a deep appreciation and love for each other based on what each has given to the other through the events of life. The net result is almost universal survival and growth of joy in marriage.

A couple in our society married for a long time can use the experience of life together in the same way. If you did not have the full advantage of free will on your wedding day, you can gain that advantage now. Use your years of married history to accelerate your path of joy by making a renewed free choice to be married. Start by thinking back to your wedding day. Remember that man or woman next to you at your wedding. Think of the strength, the beauty, the hopes, and the dreams that he or she brought to you that day. Remember how all of that was given to you that day. Maybe things were not perfect. Maybe you were expecting a child. But in spite of the circumstances, all of what he or she had was given to you that day. Your years together prove it. Now think about all that you have been given by your spouse since that day. A portion of that youth and probably some share of the dreams have faded. Think of all the sacrifice and love you have received and given. That is the stuff of covenant love.

Even on a day when you might wonder, *Why did I do this?* think about what you have been given. In most cases, it is much. Use that perspective to make a free will choice to love and honor that person *until death do you part.* Tell your spouse how much you love him or her and how grateful you are for the life you share. Celebration and gratitude are a much better platform than regret and pity for finding joy in life and marriage. If you need the help of a good pastor or counselor, get it. But by all means, move to that free choice to live the rest of your life in covenant love with the man or woman you married. There is joy there. I promise.

2. Are you prepared, as you follow the path of marriage, to love and honor each other for as long as you both shall live?

This question is harder in today's society. In a practical sense, people live longer and have more options. Society tends to support additional options throughout life that make lifelong fidelity more difficult. But when we are deeply in the romantic phase in those days ahead of our wedding, lifelong fidelity for most of us is not a worry. The catch is that the euphoric romance will eventually transition into a stage of disillusionment. The disillusionment usually is not so dramatic that it makes us wonder, *Why did I do this?* But most of us will have our bubble broken by reality to some degree. In our marriage preparation classes, we take advantage of witness couples who share their life experiences with the couples preparing to marry. I bring in couples ranging from the newly married to those in midmarriage with twenty years or so together to mature couples like us with over forty years of marriage. Every couple, regardless of duration of marriage, conveys the message that there will be a transition from the bliss of premarriage romance to a period of some disillusionment. All the couples apologize for delivering this sad message, but they all have interesting stories of how they hit the disillusionment wall in their own marriage. To make the disillusionment point, there is nothing like the young woman who looks like the perfect parish wife telling about the time she chose to sleep in the garage.

Making couples aware that their marriages will be more challenging than they think helps reinforce the "for better or worse" commitment to lifelong marriage. Most of the examples presented are not the marriage-breaking type. However, I go beyond those stories to convey that none of us know what is in front of us twenty years out. Life happens, and it is not always what we want. I know that in a group of twenty couples, some are going to experience the really challenging stuff. I give them a list of things that can really test a marriage. I tell them that I have seen couples experience everything on the list. I have seen couples experience the worst and remain married. I have seen couples experience much less than others and split. The difference is the existence or absence of a covenant commitment by both the man and woman. This is one commitment that absolutely takes two. One, no matter how sincere, cannot do it alone. This is so apparent after divorce. In talking through someone's story, they will say, "I really meant all that I said on my wedding day. I was fully committed and did everything I could to fulfill my vows." Most often I see evidence that they are right, but the person they married did not have the same commitment. The right words were said on the wedding day, but the commitment was not real. One committed person cannot do this alone.

The time to really test whether a man and woman are ready to make a covenant commitment is long before the wedding. This gives them time to do something about any reservations. I have had a few couples cancel weddings after really thinking through their willingness to make a commitment to an unbreakable covenant marriage. But most take time to think through honestly what they would do if a serious challenge hit years down the road. I am so grateful when I see couples think about whether they are really ready to commit to stay in the marriage no matter what. By "no matter what," I mean willingness to face whatever comes and commitment to seek whatever remedies are needed to repair the marriage. If both woman and man do this, their marriage can survive anything. If only one is in for "no matter what," they will not survive the really rough patches.

So here is my covenant commitment test. I present the following list of major challenges that happen to real couples in real life. I hope and pray that none of the couples will face any of it, but some will. I tell them that this list is something for personal reflection to take home and ponder. I challenge each person to internally decide whether they are committed to stay in the marriage they are about to make even if one of the things on the list happen in their marriage. I ask them to honestly talk about it as a couple after they have come to terms with their own internal answer. In effect, what I am doing is bringing to the table the kind of things that I see surface in postdivorce conversations. These are the conversations that happen when a person sits with me explaining what broke the marriage as he or she petitions for an annulment. Almost always the message comes out about how one spouse was not willing to try to find remedies that would make it possible to remain married.

Here are a few life events that can really test a marriage to its limits:

- substance abuse
- sexual addiction
- depression
- loss of a child
- infertility
- disability of spouse or child
- financial ruin
- dependent relatives
- infidelity

- loss of job
- conviction of a crime
- loss of faith

If there is something on this list that you know would cause you to exit marriage, you are not at the covenant point. But if you can say, "No matter what happens, I am not quitting this marriage," you are at the covenant point. Most couples I know enter marriage ready to live prepared for whatever life delivers. Thinking about possible difficult times just strengthens that commitment.

Again, it takes two. If your fiancé is not there, you do not have the foundation for an enduring covenant marriage. It is also important to understand that this does not mean that you need to stay in an abusive marriage. In that kind of marriage, you may have fully committed to the covenant at the beginning. But the life behavior of the other person in being abusive or being chronically unfaithful demonstrates that that man or woman was insincere or incapable of forming the real sacramental bond. Upon witness to what occurred before and in the marriage, the annulment process will confirm that the sacramental bond was not there. In such a case, you will have a civil divorce. However, the annulment, or decision of nullity, is not "Catholic divorce" since the annulment judgment basically says that the sacramental bond was not full. There is no such thing as Catholic divorce. Finally, it needs to be said that annulment does not affect anything that happened in a civil sense or even the so-called legitimacy of children from the marriage. There is no stamp of "illegitimate" cast on children from the marriage or any statement about things like homeownership or property. All children are treasures and gifts from God.

In view of what I just wrote about rocks that can jeopardize a marriage, your mood might be tempered at this point. That is not where I want you to be. The news from this covenant test and grim mediation really is good. I have witnessed couples who experienced some terrible things remain married because they stayed with it and worked hard to save their marriage. They probably have more joy now than they ever knew before. Attend a gathering of long married couples. You will certainly hear a few stories from people who can witness that survival is possible after any disaster. Coming through a crisis and remaining committed to marriage brings immense joy. There is so much more to be had on that path than quitting. But again, it takes two. If you can determine before your wedding day that you and your fiancé are committed no matter what, you are good to form a rock-solid covenant marriage. The covenant commitment makes all the difference.

So are you prepared to stay in your marriage and work to repair whatever needs to be repaired no matter what? Is the person you are about to marry willing to do the same? If you both answer yes, you are forming a covenant marriage. This is a *really* good way to start a marriage.

3.   Are you prepared to accept children lovingly from God and to bring them up according to the law of Christ and his church?

This is a question where the answer lurks deeper in the hearts of the man and woman than the first two questions. In modern society where having children is not a given for married couples, it may take years to see whether the man and woman really meant it when they said yes to openness to children. I cannot remember a person in marriage preparation saying that they were not open to having children. Yet away from the scrutiny of the church, I hear young couples say they do not plan to have children. This is a choice I respect but am saddened to hear. The intensity of career and wealth creation and the pleasures they bring do not last. There will be a day when the career is over and absence of family will rob that man and woman of much joy.

More common is the apparent movement apart of a woman and man in marriage over the matter of having children or how many children to have as their marriage matures. I wonder how many have changed their desire for children over their years together compared to how many had unspoken diverse attitudes about openness to children before marriage. This is a very sad circumstance to see two people committed to a marriage where there is disagreement about this fundamental purpose of marriage. This topic makes solid grounds for marriage counselling. More often, the matter stays as a lingering hurt in a marriage where joy is forever dampened or the marriage ends in divorce.

A key step in the path to joy in marriage is coming to full agreement about openness to children before marriage. If there is a difference, the marriage should not happen. In a sacramental sense, if the marriage is made with open objection to openness to children by one or both people, the marriage lacks a critical component to be sacramental. In such a marriage, the answer of yes to the question during the wedding is a lie. If divorce happens, this lie is strong grounds for annulment of what looked like a marriage.

In Pope Paul VI's teaching, *Humane Vitae,* the document most known for making a strong moral stand against artificial contraception, he described the "twofold significance of the marriage act" as the "inseparable connection between the unitive significance and the procreative significance of the marriage act."[16] These words are critically important to our life in marriage. In using the words "marriage act," he is clearly talking about sexual intercourse. He tells us there are two moral components of the sex act that are aligned with the divine plan. These two components ring loudly from the words of those first chapters of Genesis. These two components provide a test for any couple to use to guide them morally in their marital sex life. As married people having sex, we can look at anything we might be thinking of doing through two lenses. First, is the act something that will bring more unity in all ways to our marriage? Second, is the act open to forming new life? As I will discuss more in the section on the joy of sex within marriage, there is little in the Catholic Catechism regarding dos and don'ts of sex within marriage beyond this two-component test. If a man or woman enters marriage consciously closed to their sexual relations forming new life, their marriage lacks one of the two basic parts of marriage.

Not everyone is cut out to be parents. There are reasons that a couple may not be able to have children. But if two people come to marriage closed to having children, the marriage should not happen. If a man or woman is not fully honest with their fiancé about openness to children, the marriage is based on a sad lie and heartbreak will be the result. But if a man and woman enter marriage recognizing that a core purpose is bringing new life to humanity, immense joy will come. I see endless witnesses to the joy that comes from family. Please think about the answer to this covenant making

---

[16] Pope Paul VI, Encyclical, *"Humanae Vitae,"* 12, 1968

question well ahead of your wedding. Don't just make this an automatic based on what the church wants to hear. Be sure you and your fiancé are aligned in the deep-felt commitment behind your answer of yes to new life at your wedding.

The Consent: Your Vows

Following the three questions, the minister will ask the woman and man to join hands and declare their consent before the church and God. Unlike the movies where vows are open to practically any words the couple wishes, the church has words that are carefully formed to reflect consent to a covenant. There are several forms in the rite, but all have the same basic substance.

The bridegroom says,

> I, N., take you, N., to be my wife.
> I promise to be faithful to you,
> in good times and in bad,
> in sickness and in health,
> to love you and to honor you
> all the days of my life.

The bride says,

> I, N., take you, N., to be my husband.
> I promise to be faithful to you,
> in good times and in bad,
> in sickness and in health,
> to love you and to honor you
> all the days of my life.

In these words, the couple commits to a true covenant. The words include promises of fidelity no matter what. No one knows what life will dish out, but by these words, the couple promises each other that nothing will cause them to move away from the covenant until it is fully completed at the end of their lives. These words add depth of how the man and woman will live in marriage to the questions before consent. The earlier "before consent" questions establish the ability to make a covenant, the free will question, and the commitment to the twin essentials of marriage: unity and openness to life. The consent words, or what most would recognize as vows, commit to a way of life. Beyond fidelity, the promise to love and honor brings a commitment to selfless giving to the other modeled after our Lord. The words mean that things like bullying or manipulative behavior have no place. Lack of respect or lack of full openness on all matters has no place. There will be no hiding finances or relationships from the other. There will be putting the spouse first ahead of other friends or family of origin. These words form the foundation for being a full partner for the good of each other in every practical part of life.

In this book, the chapters that follow deal with practicalities of differences in personality, money, sex, family bonds, parenting, and living faith. All presume a commitment to the promises of this consent or vows. The intent in sharing experience pertaining to those topics is to give you useable tools and ideas to find more joy in living out your marriage promises. As a clergyman, it is very important that I go beyond preaching and do all that I can do to help couples live the challenges of marriage in a way that joy will be theirs. I have confidence that our church is solidly on this page. That is why this covenant making happens in public. At its best, covenant making happens before humanity and God in the bride's and/or groom's local parish with an entire congregation ready to help them live up to their promises.

After the words of consent (vows), there are the public signs that seal the covenant, such as an exchange of rings, a kiss, and possibly an exchange of cultural symbols, such as *arras* (coins). But the biggest sign of a true covenant commitment remains ahead as the couple lives in marriage. A couple that has really taken to heart the words of this day will find joy beyond what they imagined on their wedding day. That joy will show itself to the world as a great witness to God's divine plan and gift of marriage.

Chapter 4

THE PERFECT THREESOME: MAN, WOMAN, AND GOD

Another key element of the marital road to joy is faith. God was a partner in our marriage from the beginning. We appreciate that there are things beyond our control. When things really seem beyond our limits, there has always been hope. We also recognize that our marriage is a gift from God. It is a gift as part of the eternal plan for humanity as well as a gift in the sense of the mysterious wonder of how we found each other. Our faith tells us to remember our tiny place in eternity and fully recognize the wonder of God. As part of that wonder, we are called to recognize and be good stewards of what God gives us. Marriage is one of those gifts—a very big gift—to be nurtured as we would other gifts from God. In that sense, we humbly thank God for this marriage and look to him to strengthen us as we live out a covenant of love for each other and for the God who made us.

Marriage does take care and nurturing. Stuff happens in every marriage. There are good days and bad days. Our faith and experience of life tell us that God will not abandon us. Looking back on over forty years of marriage, we know that with two simple things—faith and a covenant commitment—joy is there. Faith will not make the hurt of bad times go away, but it will make the road back to joy certain and much faster.

There are books that focus on a theological approach to marriage. These often use a Trinitarian model. As in the Trinity, marriage is composed of three persons alive in one marriage. In this model, husband and wife become one enlivened by the presence of God. Each remains a unique person but becomes one in marriage. This book is not a theological masterpiece and thus will not go deeper in this model. Instead, this section looks at life as three persons—man, woman, and God—living as one united in a covenant relationship. The focus here is on how to practically grow that relationship in marriage.

Marriage is hard. There are difficult times that crush many couples, yet other couples come through. God gives us many gifts, including wisdom and talents that allow us to accomplish many things and overcome many hardships. Many times, we are called to use our gifts to work through challenges of life. God does not have everything precooked, treating us as puppets. We have free will and talents that we are obligated to honor and use. Faith does not mean simply telling God, "This looks tough. You handle it." We are expected to be active in this. But there are times when we are at our limits. That's when we need to live the intent of these words in the Lord's Prayer: "Lead us not into temptation." Those words are not simply "God, don't play games with us by leading us into tempting spots." The words mean, "Don't take us beyond our limits." Those words have deep meaning for us in marriage. In marriage, we do face the wall now and then. In those times, who can we turn to or trust other than God? That is when it is so good to have him in our marriage. In our marriage, he has had a knack of being there when we really needed him. I remember times with a deathly ill child or even facing a difficult life decision when I know he carried us through.

I see the greatest evidence of God giving deliverance when I witness couples facing what seem to be impossible challenges. In spite of great challenges, they prevail with joy through faith. A couple that helps us with marriage preparation has six kids, works hard, but does not have wealth. I know they do not have a normal amount of worldly resources to meet what I know a family needs. Yet they are amazing. In a secular sense, I don't know how they make it. Yet their faith is deep, and they witness always to the presence of God in their lives. They openly attest that they don't know where the next dollar or answer will come from, but God delivers.

I admire their faith and simplicity. God's work is obvious in them. They have a joy that I do not see in other couples who have much more wealth, talent, and other measurable stuff.

In marriage, we need God for the ordinary as well as the hard times. In normal times as we meet day-to-day challenges, we can handle most of what comes our way. People without faith do that just fine. Most days they can say, "I don't need God. I can handle it." But for people of faith, we can feel the presence of God through even our normal experiences like the joy of our children or how we feel the joy of life at the end of a good day. We feel him with us every day. This awareness plus prayer nurtures an everyday relationship with God. By prayer, I most refer to the almost continuous dialogue with God that happens many times each day. This usually is not the formal words of prayer we learned as kids. It is the conversation that happens between grownups about what is going on in life. It is the type of conversation that happens between intimate friends. Many of the informal prayers ask for help with tasks as they come. Many of the prayers are also prayers of thanksgiving for the everyday answers and help that we get.

With this type of ongoing relationship, we are positioned to know that he is there when we are challenged beyond our limits. It is at those times that we have an immense advantage over couples without God in their marriage. We have confidence to know that we will get through the challenge and that there will be joy on the other side. It is when we are most challenged that we discover that all things are possible with God. This does not mean life will be easy. It also does not mean that we will be spared every hurt and tragedy. Sometimes the lifeline we need from God is just to carry us through. In a parish mission I led, a woman, Barbara is her name, witnessed on the topic of miracles. She spoke under the theme of "I believe in miracles, but I don't know who gets them." She told the story of an event that shook her island community almost thirty years ago. The high school volleyball team was returning from a game on another island. When their plane did not appear after what should have been a short flight, the entire community turned to prayer hoping for some miracle. But that did not happen. The plane hit a mountainside and all were killed, including Barbara's daughter. This woman's faith is strong today, and she serves many grieving families in her ministry. She witnesses to the presence of God always. Her own witness shows that even when we don't get the answer we want, God is there. She attests to the many things that came into her life after that day and spiritual connection her family feels with their daughter/sister to this day.

People like that teach me how empty life would be at tragic times without God. This is a paradox that appears in the real stuff of life. We need God most when we feel most alone and wonder where he is. It is people like this mother who teach me what no theology book can teach about the real presence of God in his creation and the love of people around us. That presence is nowhere as deep as it is in marriage. Without God in tragic times, the times are just tragic. With God, there is joy on the other side of the tragedy. There will be tragedies of some kind in your life. There will be times in your marriage when you will need him more than you can imagine.

Bringing God fully into a marriage takes more than just passively letting it happen. The inertia of our individual faith life and relationship with God can seem enough. But we grow up as individuals forming a relationship with God rooted in where we come from: our family of origin or even faith community. In most cases, the one we marry did not come from the same background. A woman and man usually come to marry from families with differences in faith tradition. Even couples like Frances and I, who both grew up Catholic, find differences. For Frances, faith was an everyday and active thing. Both parents were Catholic. In their rural community, the parish priest often had Sunday dinner at their family table. Her mother led the rosary in their home. In my case, my mother was not Catholic. On Sundays, my father took my grandmother and the kids to the earliest and shortest mass. That was followed by picking up the Sunday paper and going home to end the Communion fast. My mother then went alone to the Baptist church for her worship. In those days emanating from pre-Vatican II life, our family never experienced worship as an entire family. So even though Fran's mom looked at my arrival at that first Thanksgiving Day dinner with joy because I was Catholic, I had a grass roots experience of Catholic that was different from what Frances had. As Frances and I formed our marriage, we learned much about our joint heritage of faith and brought God into our marriage in a way that fit who we are. What we have today is not exactly like what either of us had as teens.

Since we were both Christian and Catholic, we did not have to start at ground zero in nurturing a God relationship in our marriage, but we had work to do. We knew we were going to live as active Catholics. We knew we were going to raise our children Catholic. We knew we were going to be active in church. We knew we were going to enter marriage in a chaste way and then bring natural family planning into our intimate life. There was much to build on by simply being Catholic together, but there was much yet to learn. Any couple, regardless of faith tradition, can invite God in with the result being strength and joy.

For Frances and me, as Catholics, we have the basic truths and traditions of the Catholic Church as the platform for God and faith in our marriage.

We had the basics of the "Big T" traditions we say in the creed that are core beliefs. It was the "small t" traditions that we had to develop describing how we live our beliefs. Things like form and amount of prayer together. Things like icons in our house and devotions. Things like learning more about our faith. These are the things that help a couple advance their inclusion of God in daily life of marriage in a personal and special way. These are the things that paid off later when challenges hit.

With the reality that husband and wife often come from different traditions, couples coming to marry need to allow the faith dimension of marriage to grow like any other part of marriage. The starting place is to openly make a place for God in marriage. Agreeing to prepare for a faith community celebration of marriage in a church is a good place to start. As such, you will have access to the church community to help you prepare to marry. In your marriage preparation, you have a chance to talk about prayer and faith traditions in a way that will help you find ways to openly include faith in your married life. In a church marriage preparation program, you probably will have or had some kind of workbook to help build this faith platform. Those workbooks are excellent tools to help you reflect on where you and your spouse-to-be come from in faith. What is in the heads of the two of you when it comes to a living relationship with God? What do you hope will carry over into your marriage? Spend time working on this. Use some of that dreamy time before marriage, when you're pondering life, to build the details of your faith life together.

One special part of that faith life together is prayer. Prayer is absolutely essential in marriage. But each couple will find a different prayer style. Some couples will do everything together, such as saying the rosary together or studying scripture together. They find great joy in this togetherness. Other couples will have more diversity due to different backgrounds and even different personality types. Frances and I tried complete togetherness in prayers and found that each of us had different needs. As a deacon, I say the daily prayers of the church, the daily "office." We tried doing that together, and it just did not feel natural. Now we spend prayer time together, but it is in chairs next to each other using different forms. I use the formal prayers. Frances uses meditation guides and scripture. We feel the presence of God together but experience it through different tools. For us, this actually is a gift giving us the chance to compare our different experiences as we wrap up meditations.

The important point here is to include frequent prayer in your marriage. Depending on your background, this may not be easy. The intimacy of prayer together is much more difficult to attain than the physical intimacy of sex. In prayer, our most profound weaknesses and failings come into the open. This is very hard to do with another human being. However, the flip side of this reality is that as we pray together, we build intimacy that strengthens the bond and pays off in other parts of the marriage. Prayer is a vehicle that can bring our greatest worries and emotions into the open as we present them to God. If we do that together with our spouse, the three-party unity gives us strength and confidence to take on whatever life delivers. In most cases, these deep needs presented in prayer are shared needs of the couple. Prayer can make a couple experiencing hard times feel less alone. The husband and wife are not just taking on the world together; they are doing it with God as a partner. This partnership can make desperate times turn into hopeful times based on shared faith.

While it is challenging for most couples to really come to a comfort zone in shared prayer, it is worth the work. The faith background you bring into the marriage is the platform to build upon. Begin by bringing traditions that you enjoyed as you matured and share those with your fiancé. Most people probably had some form of meal grace in their homes. That is a good place to start. A second good step is awareness of thanks for gifts given. Incorporate the words "I am thankful for …" in your prayer vocabulary. Then begin to bring awareness of need and informal petition with the words "I am worried about and praying for …" These steps incorporate the divine into what is a natural course of life. As comfort builds, work together to find the best of the best leading to new prayer traditions that will be core to your marriage and family. Talk about it now ahead of your marriage, and be prepared for evolution and growth in this intimate part of your lives.

There is much more that could be said about forming a strong faith platform in your marriage. I will leave much of that to your own exploration as you find ways to include God in your marriage.

The last point I do want to bring in is the importance of being part of a faith community. Living faith is not a solo sport. It cannot be done without God, and it is meant to be lived as a community. Jesus simplified the commandments down to loving God and loving neighbor. As people of faith, we do this by worshiping together. Often people will suggest, "I don't need church. I have my own relationship with God." That's like saying, "I don't need a husband. I can adopt a kid anytime I need." People actually do live that way, but it is so incomplete. In our days of leading marriage preparation in London, I asked the couples, "Why are you coming to the church for your wedding?" I told them, "I like to run. Every Saturday I run past the Westminster City Hall, and there are happy couples coming out full of joy newly married. They look as happy as couples that I see coming out of our church. Why bother with a church wedding?"

The best answer I got was from a Czech-born atheist who was marrying a Catholic. He said, "Marriage is hard. I see support in this faith community that is going to help us be successful living our marriage." That was a remarkable answer from a man who had not experienced the reality of God. He is absolutely right. When I witness a marriage, just before I invite the couple to come forward to exchange vows and form a sacramental marriage, I tell those present, "As Catholics, we celebrate sacraments in public because our faith is lived as a community. We are called to live as a community and live in love for each other." I then say, "You may have been raised being told that you must be quiet in a Catholic church. This is not one of those times. Express with all your voice and energy: are you ready to do all you can to help this woman and this man, who are about to profess their love before us, live their lives true to the promises they are about to make?" I expect and always get a resounding yes!

Living a lifelong marriage is not always easy. But it is much easier with God as part of it and with the support of a faith community. The support of the community is always there. It is up to each of us as married couples to decide to take advantage of it. Your wedding day is a very good time to recommit to being an active part of a community. When you do, this is just the beginning of a long series of very good times that come from your membership in a church. You will experience the support of young adult faith groups that combine fun with help with the real challenges of early married life. You will experience the joy and support that come when your child is baptized. You will experience the support in meeting life's challenges as your family grows in faith. Through all of this, you will get the added benefit of a community that can help with the many secular challenges of life. The help may be as far reaching as a parochial school education for your children or as simple as help finding a babysitter when you need one.

Living with God as a full partner in your marriage will be a strength and joy. Make this a priority.

Chapter 5

THE TWO BECOME ONE
BUT WITH BAGGAGE:
FAMILY OF ORIGIN

From the beginning, God presented marriage as the ultimate form of unity. Two persons completely become one body. It happens physically, emotionally, and spiritually. During the romance phase of a relationship, becoming one seems easy. We see what we want to see and discount what we'd rather not see. For Frances and me, everything seemed aligned. When our pastor reviewed the results of our premarriage inventory with us, he said, "You conned the test," because everything was so aligned. Well, we did not con the test in the sense of answering together or consciously putting what we thought the church wanted to hear. But we did con the test out of ignorance. The ignorance was the blissful simplicity of our limited time together and intensity of our romance.

When I review the results of these types of profiles with couples now, I am happy to see alignment on the big issues needed to enter a covenant. But I am not happy when I see an almost absolute agreement showing no issues whatsoever. There are certain questions on the tool I use[17] that are clues that the couple has not fully opened their eyes to the other. Questions like "Is there anything that annoys me about my spouse-to-be" give some degree of measure on how open the couple has been to each other. When a

---

[17] FOCCUS Premarriage Inventory, FOCCUS Inc., USA, Omaha, Nebraska

person can look at the other in this kind of interview and say things like "I wish you would put down your cell phone when we eat," they are at a level for meaningful communication about their needs. Cleaning up or putting things away are the little things that can build up to issues over time. It is important at the front end of marriage to discuss even the nonromantic, trivial matters of living before differences become a big deal. Much of this little stuff, or habitual stuff, was learned in the family we came from. Everything that happened in our home can seem so normal that it becomes hard to imagine that life could be different in another family.

A task I ask couples to do is for each to create a "life map." This is just a simple drawing or collection of pictures representing the path of life from childhood to the present. A life map uses words or symbols to represent important things that have been part of a person's life. As an example, here are the maps that Frances and I prepared to describe our lives leading to our wedding day. I used pictures from our family photo albums while Frances did some stick figure drawing to tell her story. We give you these examples to show two ways that a life map can be made.

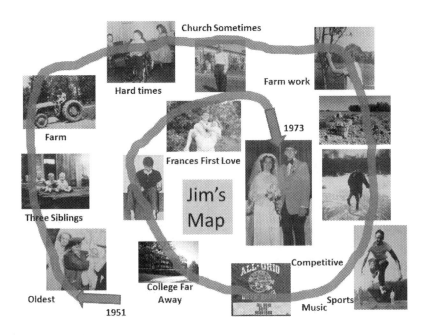

My map shows things like scenes from our farm and my dad's unsuccessful attempt at a chicken business. There is the First Communion picture that represents the occasional nature of our family Catholic faith experience. There are signs of competitiveness. There is a picture of my siblings and me as the oldest of four kids. There are symbols of music, sports, and academics.

Anyone could learn a lot about me from this map. Someone seeing this would correctly guess that I am an introvert. There are not any pictures of parties or big groups. From the map, someone could see the Catholic presence but only in one limited picture and guess that the church was not a big part of my growing up. The map shows me as the oldest of several siblings and suggests that I am someone who likes to be in charge. There are no signs of luxury hinting that I am someone with little exposure to the finer things of society, so if you're looking for polish, I'm not likely to be the one. Also apparent would be signs of someone with direction and drive from pictures of working on farms and later in mines. There are hints of someone with a passion for adventure from images representing going far away to college. All of this leads to the happy picture of me with Frances in my arms months before our wedding. Without a lot of narrative, these pictures say a lot about the baggage Frances got when she married me. If I had prepared this for Frances during our engagement, she would have learned much about me that really did not come out for years.

The map Frances prepared of her life has many elements common to mine but with important and telling differences. On her map is evidence of church showing the parish's rotund priest at dinner or family saying the rosary at home. My map does not show anything like that. My mother was Baptist, and we never went to church as a complete family. Frances's map shows a big family with siblings. But she is in the middle. I am the oldest. Her map shows the same college that I attended, but what we experienced at that college was very different. Frances lived at home and commuted daily while I was over a thousand miles from home. I competed in sports and pursued an engineering degree driven by the anticipated financial reward. Frances studied her beloved math and was immersed in books. Her map, like mine, shows a farm. But my farm experience was wildly different from hers. Her family ranch was large and successful while my family chicken farm failed. We can see in her map their *little house on the prairie* and one-room school that she attended for her first eight grades. We see evidence of what a farm girl was supposed to do: sew and cook. All of these show simplicity early in life. We see her teen years' experience from the Cold War presence of the Air Force with B-52s and nuclear missiles all around their South Dakota ranch that eventually gave her a much broader picture of the world than I got in my small Ohio town. All of these things shaped her life in ways similar to and different from me. These maps provide a basis to explore all of that together, even though we were far apart growing up.

As we prepared to marry, everything looked aligned. Forty-six years out, we know better. These differences within what seemed to be common backgrounds coming into marriage made much more difference as the years went on. For example, within the first year of our marriage, my strong competitiveness came to the forefront. I was intensely competitive at work. I brought those emotions home. Also, this led to an early disruption in the tranquility and stability Frances imagined when I got a job transfer to another state within a year of marriage. The woman who imagined life in Oklahoma to be somewhat like her South Dakota upbringing was shocked to learn that this marriage would bring a very different and less stable path. In the first five years, differences in economic circumstances in our families of origin came via financial needs and turmoil from my extended family.

In those early years after our wedding day, we did not have any tool, like this life map, to help us find the causes of some of the tensions that surfaced. If we had prepared maps like these as we prepared to marry or even early in our marriage, the images would have triggered conversation on some of the things important to us as a couple. We could have found things that shaped us in ways more different from what we imagined. In retrospect, we would have enjoyed exploring the differences since we really lived some very different and interesting paths. It would have been fun to learn all we could about each other during that romantic discovery time.

Beyond the images themselves, talking about life maps can bring out important things that are core to values and habits of daily life that matter in marriage. For example, when problems hit, did people in your family tend to shout and argue all the time or go silent? Were you the one always in charge or the one being taken care of? Were times easy or hard? What did your family do for fun? What was your family social life like? The maps tend to bring out the truth as our life actions speak more about who we are than words.

I encourage you as a couple to make a pair of maps and talk about them. A couple committed to each other for life needs every tool possible to make that road easier and more joy filled. A pair of life maps prepared by wife and husband can provide a good platform to discover differences that matter. Preparing life maps at a time when you are not at a stress point lets conversations happen about differences at a time when the discovery can be deep and fun rather than stressful. How you do it is not important. Yours may be photos or just stick figures. The art does not matter. What you need is enough imagery to trigger conversation. The longer you are married, the greater the depth that will likely appear on your maps.

Looking at the family legacy that you bring into your marriage is important because this baggage will not go away. A social scientist by the name of Morris Massey, who gained fame in the 1970s, provided a team-building method that my company used then. The method has a title based on the idea that "You are what you were when."[18] Through the 1970s, Dr. Massey was an associate dean and professor of marketing at the University of Colorado at Boulder. Core to his method is the idea that our basic personality is shaped in the early years of life. He described early development of the values that shape us. He says that up to the age of seven, we are like sponges absorbing everything around us and accepting much of it as true, especially when it comes from our parents. This is a big part of the baggage we bring to marriage. Dr. Massey described a later period, between the ages of eight and thirteen, during which we copy people, often our parents. Again, this period loaded us up with baggage to carry into our marriage. In his work, he shows that only when a person experiences what he calls "a significant emotional event" is there change from what we were in those early years. In this thinking, a marriage is not ordinarily of the magnitude to create a radical change in who and what we are.[19] We bring that former self into marriage.

Use the life map to identify and talk about some of the big things that matter from your backgrounds. Talk about the similarities and differences and what those mean to your marriage. What were you like when you were six or ten years old? How about your spouse? What was going on in your lives? The life map discussion will help you focus on some of the core experiences that will form the foundation of your life as a couple in marriage.

Beyond this foundation are many details that will comprise life as a couple that will be influenced by your family of origin. Some of these practical details, like where are you going to spend your first married Christmas, will come sooner than you think and matter more than you think. A good

[18] "Morris Massey," https://en.wikipedia.org/wiki/Morris_Massey, Last edited on 23 July 2019
[19] Changing Minds.org, "Values Development," http://changingminds.org/explanations/values/values_development.htm, 2019

marriage preparation workbook can help stimulate conversation on these matters. Check out options with the help of your church or faith-based bookstore.

A partial list of challenges from different family backgrounds follows:

- holiday traditions
- extended family visits
- assistance from parents
- gift giving
- saving
- vacations
- entertainment
- where to live
- churchgoing
- when to have kids
- size of family
- career expectations
- buying cars, homes
- sex: taboo or a fact of life
- saying sorry
- and many more!

These topics are fun to talk about and contribute to developing your ability as a couple to talk about anything. It is much easier to talk about these things before you are faced with doing something in crisis mode as a couple. You will face times when you will need to choose between divergent paths inherited from your families of origin. With rich discussion ahead of time, your path will be much clearer than choosing from legacy options in the midst of crisis. Your path will be one that you create as a couple drawing from your joint heritage but becoming something better than the parts.

The challenges family of origin create will be different for every couple. Circumstances, such as how close you live to extended family, will make a big difference. For Frances and me, we never lived closer than four hundred miles to any extended family. We had considerable freedom in forming our own traditions. Couples who live literally next door to their parents will have less freedom. That is not all bad. There were many times when it would have been wonderful to have family close by when our house was filled with young children and as our parents aged.

Thinking about family of origin is a foundation for topics like financial differences, communication, and problem-solving that are critically important to marriage. As we enter marriage, our starting place is what we bring from the family we came from. We are what we were when we were growing up. From then on, we make our own history and styles.

Given diverse backgrounds, a bottom-line challenge couples face is to come to a "we point" in marriage. This is easy for some and very hard for others. Through your marriage, you will be challenged at times to make hard choices between something important to your extended family, usually siblings or parents, and something important to your spouse. This can be especially challenging if you are entering a second marriage and bringing children into the marriage. You will face the delicate task of making a very emotional decision that will force you to get to the core of who you and your spouse are. You will be digging into the "what you were when" substance for both of you.

Occasionally, I encounter someone who is in a marriage where one person really has not left the family of origin. For most days, that can make life easy thanks to practical family support in many ways. There will be a well-established social network. There will be babysitters and always things to do. There will always be people who understand you and take your side even when your spouse is not around. But remaining more deeply attached to the family you come from is a recipe for disaster. I remember a woman who came to me for help who seemed to be from the perfect family. The family bond among parents, siblings, and beyond was remarkable. They all still lived close to each other and shared daily life almost continuously. This woman married a successful man who supported a comfortable lifestyle. They decided to make their home where the woman grew up. His job usually took him away five days a week, but the job and travel allowed the lifestyle of her family to become the lifestyle of their marriage. Externally all looked wonderful until the day she found that he was having sex with women in the cities where he worked. Obviously his actions were not right, but when I looked at the marriage, there was a deep problem in how complete the movement of the couple from two lifestyles to one actually was. She was able to continue living in the family she came from while he mainly enabled that lifestyle. The transition to a "we point" never happened. It took a crisis to force a choice to get the common point or quit. A bit to my surprise, there was mutual desire to get counselling and repair the marriage. They actually did have enough love and covenant intent to make the repairs needed to go on. Part of their future included moving to another state, where they could be together much more as a couple. As far as I know more than a decade later, they have a good marriage.

Up to this point, this discussion of baggage from family of origin focused on things that affect our behavior. The final point I need to make is a practical one. The baggage we bring into marriage includes the people we love, even are stretched to love. This includes siblings and other relatives who draw on a couple in tangible ways. For many couples, including Frances and me, this includes relatives moving in with you. It also includes financial aid in the form of loans or gifts from you. As early as you can, honestly talk with your fiancé or spouse about extended family and what kind of demands might come over the years. In more families than not, some challenge like this happens. Think ahead of time how you will approach this injection of extended family into your domestic space. If it is happening to you now, remember to keep your spouse first: now and always. He or she is your covenant partner. Not anyone else. Not even the most beloved and needy sibling or parent. This sometimes takes strength and discomfort but needs to happen in a loving way. Working together, man and woman can discover and do the difficult things that need to happen. Like all crises in marriage, the couple that does this well will come out stronger than ever. In your marriage, whatever the challenge turns out to be, think and act in favor of your marriage. The result will be a source of strength because you prevailed together.

Families and the traditions we come from are wonderful, but they bring baggage that can weigh us down in marriage. With conscious effort to join the better of two traditions, a marriage will be better than the sum of the parts. You will find joy in the life you build together beyond what you ever could find on your own.

Chapter 6

THE TWO BODIES BECOME ONE BODY WITH TWO INHERITED PERSONALITIES

The statement I make in the title of this section seems blatantly obvious. Of course we remain two personalities, but the degree that those personality differences affect our marriage is not obvious on our wedding day. For Frances and me, it took almost thirty years to figure out how our personality differences were affecting our marriage. Initially we were so locked up in the romance phase that the differences were glossed over in the blissful emotions of those days. Later, we felt that since we had been with each other for so many years, what else was there to know? If we did not understand each other by then, we never would. But then the light went on. Thanks to facilitating marriage preparation sessions and using personality tools available to our marriage preparation couples, we gained useful insight into what made us who we each are and how those differences affect our life together. Understanding those differences made our lives much better.

One of the great gifts of working to prepare couples for marriage is that we learn something every year that helps our own marriage. We learn from the couples and from the session content. One of the greatest finds was an awareness of the effect of our individual underlying personality preferences on our marriage. During my thirty years in business, as well as years preparing to become a deacon, I was subjected to numerous personality inventories. I was given personality assessment tools individually for self-improvement as well as a component of team building sessions. Over the years, I benefited from many tools. One I already mentioned is Morris Massey's *What You Are Is What You Were When*. That process drove home that we generally shape our personality early in life. Like it or not, we largely are what we are or—as Massey says—"were when." As such, we need to look back at where and what we were in our early years. Someone growing up in a family without money and endless hard times formed in a different way than someone who got anything they wanted. Frances and I grew up with different circumstances that affected what each of us has become. Talking about those differences has helped us understand each other better.

Components of this reality of differing backgrounds come up all the time in premarriage sessions. I see the differences most clearly during review of individual results from personality and readiness questionnaires. Different attitudes about money, problem solving, and even faith are sometimes profound. The explanation for these differences almost always comes back to what happened in his or her childhood and family. While I do not formally use any of the Massey methods in my work, what I know of his research shows through as true and matters. We are what we were when we were growing up. People bring their family of origin into marriage. This is baggage good and bad. The bad is sometimes very clear, including some things we wish we'd left behind.

In various team-building workshops, I have experienced many methods to identify personality preferences or characteristics that influence behavior. Some are four-box methods, while others use color schemes to label preferences. The method that has consistently brought the most to individual and team assessments is the Myers-Briggs Type Indicator® (MBTI®). The method was developed by Katherine Briggs and daughter Isabel Briggs Myers. My first encounter with their tools came via team-building workshops with the large industrial company I worked for in the 1970s. It was not just my company that used this tool; interest broadly blossomed in the 1980s in many sectors as global competition forced companies to use talent better. The importance of diversity and understanding individuals as individuals gained attention because it made a difference to bottom-line company performance. Understanding of individuals and their differences matters even more in marriage.

I highlight the use of the MBTI as the platform for this section for several reasons. First, it is the most credible and easy-to-use tool that I know of to get an understanding of the personality drivers behind the two people making a marriage. Second, MBTI results are easy to get. Many churches and groups have access to this tool. Associated with the availability of an MBTI assessment, there are even more resources online to help someone understand their personality type. Also, many people have already had an MBTI assessment via education or work so many people coming to marriage preparation workshops likely have their personal MBTI results already.

By highlighting MBTI in this book, I want to bring MBTI "type" language into your marriage as a tool to make your marriage stronger and more joy filled. In our marriage preparation sessions, we work with a trained individual certified in use of the MBTI who can access and administer the tool. Over the years working with this personality type indicator, I have experienced it as so helpful that I personally dedicated the time to become certified in its use. In marriage preparation, I use this tool as a core part of our module on communication. In marriage enrichment, it is critical as a foundation for other tools to help an already married couple understand how they each experience the same things but internalize them differently.

Output from scoring of a person's response to each of the MBTI questions generates a four-letter personality type indicator. We use this as the platform for our module on communication because communication is more than just forming and conveying words. The same words can be said or received by husband and wife with very different meanings underpinned by their individual personality characteristics or preferences. We use MBTI because it has an enduring track record of helping people and groups better understand themselves and each other. Having experienced the MBTI many times over three decades, I find it very consistent, valid, and repeatable. When discussing results of groups, I ask who has done the MBTI before. Usually, there are many who have. I ask who got the same result they got last time they did the MBTI. Most report the same result as before.

In our marriage, any time I participated in use of some personality assessment tool at work, I brought the results home and discussed them with Frances. Most of the time, what I presented did not convince her that doing something like those tests and tools could benefit us. Somewhere after thirty years of marriage, we took the MBTI and compared our results in the context of what we were saying to the couples preparing for marriage. We discovered that there are some significant differences between us in our basic personality wiring. Suddenly, we had an awareness of why we struggle to say things to each other. We discovered why we sometimes say things that bring on emotions that are not intended. We gained a language to help us understand each other better that gave us a significant boost in our marital joy. We do not want any other couple to wait thirty years to discover what we found using MBTI. Based on our experience personally and help we have given others, we believe that even couples married for decades can improve their marriage significantly using this personality type information. Please take this MBTI step!

The MBTI looks at the following four dimensions of our individual personality preferences:

- Where we receive and direct our energy: Do our ideas and actions form from energy within ourselves or from energy drawn from those around us?
- How we take in information from what we experience: Is the focus simply on what we take in with our senses face value, or is the focus based on our assessment of implications that could result based on what we experience?

- Basis for our decisions: Do we depend on logic or depend on emotion?
- How we approach the outside world and build the path for our life: Are answers to the issues of life clear or wide-open with possibilities?

The MBTI uses a "letter" label for contrasts within each of the four categories. Based on a series of questions, the tool provides feedback on an individual's tendency within each category to prefer one end versus the other. The contrasts are the following:

- where we receive and direct our energy: extravert (E) versus introvert (I)
- how we take in information from what we experience: sensor (S) versus intuitive (N)
- basis for our decisions: thinking (T) versus feeling (F)
- how we approach the outside world and build our path of life: judging (J) versus perceiving (P)

Using the four contrasts and two letters for each, there are a total of sixteen personality types. These can be conveyed as a grid showing the full range of personality types.

Myers Briggs Personality Preference Grid

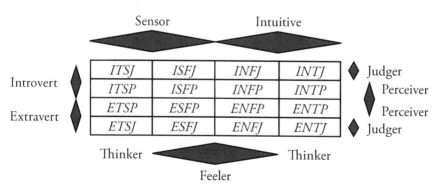

It is important to understand that no one is absolutely on one end or the other of any of the preference contrasts. We all have some element of the opposite preference. It is also important to avoid putting someone in a category box identified by any of the letters. A person is not an I or an E or an S or an N. Their personality makeup includes components of each preference. What the letters indicate is a person's tendency for using one preference versus the other. In the section that follows, I violate the purity of this advice in several sections. For simplicity, I will use words that can imply that I believe that a person can be defined by one letter or another using language like I or E. In places where I do that, I am merely trying to avoid having to say words like "person with a preference for" as I discuss each preference. Please know that when I do that it is a literal shortcut and not intended to be a way to define any human being. Saying that a person is an introvert, a sensor, or a judger is a shorthand way for me to describe someone with a particular personality preference. We are all complex human beings who have developed preferences that impact who we are but not creatures so extreme in any preference that we can be defined by that. We are too complex to be defined by any letter-defined box. However, awareness of our preferences described by the four letters of MBTI makes a big difference in experiencing joy in marriage.

Recently I found results published by the career placement company CareerPlanner.com showing distribution of people tested by their firm in terms of the MBTI.[20] They tested several hundred thousand people and presented a profile of that community by personality type. The data show what we see in our local sessions. The world is made up of people representing each of the sixteen types. The data also shows that the distribution is not equal. Some types are much more common than others. There is also a difference between men and women.

Just like the world as measured by CareerPlanner.com, we have a diversity of types in our marriage preparation sessions. It surprises our groups how diverse they are. Even though our groups are largely from one region, generally from similar social backgrounds in a small-town environment,

[20] Michael T. Robinson, *"How Rare is Your Personality Type,"* https://www.careerplanner.com/MB2/TypeInPopulation.cfm, As presented July 26, 2019

and share some connection to Catholicism, they come with an amazing range of personality types. The value of diversity is strongly apparent as the couples appreciate each other. The groups generally are made up of people representing nearly every type. In a room full of good people, it is easy to appreciate the existence and value of the differences. Clearly every type is valuable to our life in community and church. Understanding personality types for the people we meet enhances our ability to see and understand those around us—especially those most important to us like our wife or husband. In a community, understanding these differences matters. In marriage, understanding the differences in personality preference or type between wife and husband is critical.

Hopefully you will take or have taken the MBTI preference step. If not, the following discussion can be a down payment for estimating what your type preferences might be. As you read the discussion of each of the contrasts, think about which of the contrasts more fits you. Use that to make a first stab at what your preference might be. Do that for each of the four contrasts, and you will have a first estimate of your four-letter type. Again, this is not a substitute for actually taking the MBTI. Seek a source for the actual assessment. Your local community college may offer this resource. Your church is also likely to be a good place to start.

Recognizing that there are sixteen types in the world around us, it is important to look at what the contrasts mean. In this section, you will gain a look at each of the four contrasts.

Extravert (E) versus Introvert (I): Where We Receive and Direct Our Energy and Form Our Ideas and Actions

The letters of the type indicator are so ingrained in Frances and me that we often make a quiet remark after encountering someone: "Extravert" or "Introvert." The two of us have clear introvert preferences. By "clear," I mean, given the number of responses we made to the MBTI questions, we each had a large number of answers pointing toward the introvert preference. We really did not need the test to tell us this. However, the results gave us a confirmation of what we felt and some language that we can use when we are challenged to communicate.

For people with a clear introvert preference, those with an extravert preference are amazing people. We who have an introvert preference can be present in a social situation holding a drink with little to say then encounter someone who can just tell story after story without end. We wonder how he or she can even think of all they are saying. With our introvert preference, we are working over thoughts internally to form a message in the time it takes somebody with an extravert preference to deliver bundles of interesting thoughts. It is a mystifying but wonderful to experience.

Observing people with an extravert preference, some things stand out. People with an extravert preference can be popular and have many friends. They can think on the fly and at times talk then think forming ideas from words already delivered. The listener can experience the idea-forming process right before their eyes by what their ears hear. The person with an extravert preference can multitask, easily talking on the telephone while doing something else. They can be brilliant at social media, sharing all sorts of things. In work sessions, they enjoy group problem solving and work in a group. They can thrive on the energy external to them in the group.

Contrast this to someone with an introvert preference. Those with an introvert preference take time to respond. Words do not just spill out as part of the idea-forming process. There is a need to form the idea then let it loose. Internally they rehearse then talk. They enjoy private time and can be known as great listeners. To those with an extravert preference, they can seem shy and selective with friendships.

Looking at those whose preference is E or I, using the CareerPlanner.com data, the distribution of E preference and I preference in their client base is about even at 49 percent E's and 51 percent I's. That higher number also matches the general E preference population of our local marriage preparation couples. In our daily life, it is easy to experience the E versus I preference difference in the people we meet and even phone conversations. The difference also comes out in how a person presents a problem as far as how far the person has analyzed the problem before presenting it. It is harder in more structured settings to see the difference. Someone with a strong introvert preference can still be a good teacher, preacher, or presenter. He or she just needs time to prepare.

In this faith-based presentation of I and E preferences, I use an example of I's and E's in our history of faith with a little paraphrasing added. In scripture, we hear the apparently introvert-preferring Moses having a conversation with God about God's call for Moses to lead his people. Moses is reluctant. According to Exodus 4:10, "Moses, however, said to the LORD, 'If you please, my Lord, I have never been eloquent, neither in the past nor now that you have spoken to your servant; but I am slow of speech and tongue.'" Moses seems to be saying, "No, Lord, don't send me. I have never been a good speaker ..."

But the Lord responds in the next verses, Exodus 4:11–12,

> The LORD said to him: Who gives one person speech? Who makes another mute or deaf, seeing or blind? Is it not I, the LORD? Now go, I will assist you in speaking and teach you what you are to say.

But that is still not enough for an introvert. In the next verse, Moses says, "But he said, 'If you please, my Lord, send someone else!'"

Then the Lord brings out the beauty of individual strengths that come from personality differences. In Exodus 4:14, we get the answer.

> Then the LORD became angry with Moses and said: I know there is your brother, Aaron the Levite, who is a good speaker; even now he is on his way to meet you. When he sees you, he will truly be glad.

As the story of Exodus plays out in these verses, we see that Aaron had no problem speaking. He was an accomplished speaker, which is typical of someone with an extravert preference. The Lord knew how to draw on the unique types he created. Moses and Aaron, like all human beings, come with inborn and sometimes contrasting preferences here imagined as I and E!

Life is still like that. We need people with both preferences toward the introvert and extravert contrasts. In marriage, it is handy to have one spouse with an extravert preference as the "go to" person to start a conversation. In couples like Frances and me, where both husband and wife show an introvert preference, conversation can be tough at times. We may be aware of the need to talk but have difficulty in forming the words to get the communication started. The urgency to communicate is strong, but getting started can be tough when husband and wife are both equipped with an inborn I preference. I have also seen the opposite challenge come from a pair of strong E preference people. I had a recent marriage preparation conversation with a couple who both indicated their preference to be clearly E. In fact, on the MBTI answer sheet, the husband answered every question that had a bearing on the I versus E preference as indicating that he preferred E. In trying to help them discuss issues from their marriage personal inventory, my biggest challenge was finding an opening to make a point as they talked, often both at once. One of my biggest points to them was to make time to listen to each other.

Knowing the preferred style on the E versus I contrast spectrum is important in marriage. We need to understand our own preference and that of our spouse. Here are some observations:

Someone with an Extravert Preference Married to Someone with an Introvert Preference

The style of communication will be different between husband and wife. At times, there will be discomfort when the spouse with the extravert preference overwhelms the other who has the introvert preference. The one with the introvert preference will frustrate the one with the extravert preference by seeming unresponsive to ideas presented. The one with the extravert preference needs to know that the mate with the introvert preference is not ignoring or downplaying the ideas he or she has just heard. The issue is that the one showing the introvert preference needs time to form a response. Going the other way, an introvert preference spouse trying to communicate information to their extravert preference spouse will have challenges. When the spouse with the introvert preference speaks, the thought has generally been thought out. The one with the extravert preference may be able to quickly respond but needs to take enough time to provide a respectful response with the thought needed. A quick answer can feel like a dismissal to someone with an introvert preference.

An Extravert Preference Person Married to Someone with an Extravert Preference

Each is very capable of beginning a conversation. Both deliver words about ideas and issues as fast as thoughts develop. Here the challenge is listening. Each has so much to say that there is little time to assimilate and process what the other just said. In this couple, the biggest communication tool to practice is quality listening. This can begin with simple awareness of the tendency both have to respond quickly without due thought to what the other just said. With that awareness, take a breath and think before responding. On important matters, confirm and clarify by repeating back what you think you just heard.

Someone with an Introvert Preference Married to a Spouse with a Similar Introvert Preference

This is the Fran and Jim couple, so I know this one well. Both husband and wife like to internally work things out before letting any words loose. This can mean frustrating silence even when both know there is something that needs to be talked about. Since both are thoughtful people, a good and constructive conversation can happen. The catch is someone needs to start the conversation. Here it is helpful for both people to be aware of how difficult it is to bring up a hard topic. The start is tough but might include openings like "I've been thinking about …" or "You look like there is something on your mind. May I listen?"

In all these couples, being aware of communication type preferences can make life much easier. When there is a difference in style, each can help the other by drawing on their individual strength in communication style. Sometimes in ordinary communication, it is useful to use "type language" at times when the similarities or differences are causing difficult communication. Times like when the one with an introvert preference needs to bring something up but finds it hard to do. He or she can say, "You know in my introvert preference style I have trouble saying all that I want to say. But there is something I want to talk about so here it is …" The person with an extravert preference can do the same when he or she is trying to form an idea and needs to talk things out. The one with the extravert preference can say, "The extravert preference in me is trying to figure out what to do about … Can I spill my thoughts for you?"

A big benefit of doing this in routine conversation is to gain the skills before facing more challenging times, like conflict. In conflict or in an argument, the E preference will have the advantage. The one with the introvert preference can be defeated before even entering the conflict. Two with an extravert preference may shout at each other for an hour and get nowhere while two with an introvert preference will be stuck in silence. None of these situations are good, but all can be made better with awareness and practice.

What I am about to say here goes beyond just the E versus I contrast. In marriage, conflict is inevitable—especially between contrasting types. Different personality types see conflict in different ways. The challenge is magnified because no type is really good at handling conflict. But ignoring personality types is deadly in resolving conflict; it can add fuel to the fire. It is in those times that we need to be the best we can be by knowing the strengths and challenges of our own personality preference and that of our spouse. Here we can use type language and some of the tips already mentioned to ensure a constructive connection, even in the heat of conflict. This can make all the difference between joyful resolution of an issue versus angry frustration in a lingering conflict.

Sensor (S) Preference versus Intuitive (N) Preference: How We Process What We Experience

This element of personality type has a big impact on a relationship. It is big because of its impact on how we feel about what we hear or experience and what energy we put into using that input. People with a sensor (S) preference prefer specifics. They have a keen focus on the moment and what is happening in that moment. They can take things literally and convey things with clarity.

People who have an intuitive (N) preference are more general in both view of what is happening and how they communicate. Often they can have a relative view of time and space. They can think beyond what is happening now to project where events might be going. The MBTI uses *N* for intuitive since *I* was already used for introvert.

If you wonder how these differences have affected life, here scripture gives us another example of differences at work in humanity. We read in Numbers 13 the story about Moses sending spies to assess how challenging the inhabitants of the Land of Canaan would be. This piece of faith history demonstrates how different the perception of an event can be between people with apparent S and N preferences.

Twelve spies were sent out. In Numbers 13:27–28, we hear one group report,

> They told Moses: "We came to the land to which you sent us. It does indeed flow with milk and honey, and here is its fruit. However, the people who are living in the land are powerful, and the towns are fortified and very large."

This is a typical S response. They report what they saw just as they saw it.

But one of the twelve had a different take on the same observations: Two verses later, Numbers 13:30 tells us, "Caleb, however, quieted the people before Moses and said, 'We ought to go up and seize the land, for we can certainly prevail over it.'" Caleb acts like an N preference individual who could see possibilities beyond the mere observed facts. He could see the same things that the other eleven saw but could uniquely see opportunities that the others could not.

Thinking of this encounter in "type" language, we can see the differences between an S and an N report. Those who seemed to have an S preference reported (paraphrasing),

> The land is rich and fertile, there is some fruit. But the people there are tall and powerful … We saw the descendants of giants there … No, we are not strong enough to attack them."

But the spy who seemed to have an N preference reported (paraphrasing),

> The land we explored is an excellent land … Don't be afraid of the people … We will conquer them easily. The Lord is with us …

Both views were critical to the destiny of Israel. Both groups observed the same situation but reported very different stories. The S preference spy report is literal and conclusive. "No, we are not strong enough to attack them." But the N preference spy looked at the possibilities and was less concerned about the literal facts. These kind of image differences go on in our heads all the time as different people with different personality preferences observe a situation. Now consider this type of difference of view between husband and wife as two people deal with conflict or consider a situation important to a marriage.

Frances and I have a strong contrast on this characteristic. It was the MBTI that helped us finally understand why we often react in very different ways to things that seem like ordinary events or comments. Frances may tell me, "Rose called." Rose is our oldest daughter. When Frances, the one with the inborn S preference, reports this simple fact to me, I start thinking about the possibilities far beyond the simple fact that Rose called. Operating with my N preference, I am thinking, *Did Rose have a disagreement with her husband or trouble with her job? Is she sick? Does she need something?*

Frances with her S preference is merely reporting a fact. Nothing more is intended than to convey that news that Rose called. But the inborn N preference in me takes off wondering what that news means. In our case, Frances is just reporting the fact. I am taking the fact far beyond what it meant. Imagine the stress this difference can cause in marriage. There is the basic assumption that *I see it; you see it.* But we do not process what we see in the same way. We think that we see the same thing, but we don't. With different personality-driven lenses, we may not see the same or intended meaning of that event. We need the tools to understand that the personality preference lens our spouse has may be very different from our own. Awareness of MBTI preferences can provide that lens.

All living things gather information and use it. The difference in the S/N personality driver is how narrow or wide the interpretation of that information is. In our society, sensors predominate. Looking at S and N presence using the CareerPlanner.com data, 70 percent of Americans are S's. So most people we run into in America have a preference for S and take information directly as it comes to them; often their words describe what they take in. The 30 percent minority, the people with an N preference, collects information and translates it. An S preference person can see a snowstorm and say, "Looks like a good storm—about an inch an hour!" The person with an N preference sees the same snowstorm and says, "Looks like a snow day tomorrow for the kids!"

In marriage, we depend heavily on information. We get it from a large number of sources. Where the information takes meaningful shape is in our heads. Depending on which end of this S/N contrast we are, we can absorb this information in ways similar to our spouse or wildly different. Think of how different a comment about appearance or some news about a child or a job can be absorbed depending on whether it is a sensor or intuitive receiving the news. The contrast can even affect how some news is shaped and delivered to our spouse. The person with the sensor preference will tend to just report what is observed. The person with the intuitive preference will often include implications.

So here are some thoughts about how couples with shared preferences as well as couples with a mix can use this type awareness to improve their life together.

Thoughts for Two Sensor Preference People Joined in Marriage

The good news is both have a similar lens to filter information as they receive it. Both tend to take things as they are. Both should be comfortable saying what they see. This allows tangible actions to deal with tangible events. The risk is that some implications of the events may escape this couple since both are generally literal. In this couple, it would be handy to develop a habit of asking each other questions like "Are we seeing the whole picture?" or "Are we missing something here?" Obviously this is not needed on every event of the day. However, on bigger matters or major news, a look beyond the literal for possible implications can help.

Thoughts about Two People with Intuitive Preferences Joined in Marriage

The good news is that this couple has a very broad field of view. Stress can come from overthinking some things or needless worry. Also, one or the other may be thinking too hard about the impact that sharing some news may have on the other to the point that he or she hesitates to say what needs to be said. This couple needs good communication skills to facilitate constructive dialogue aimed at putting things in proper perspective and logically coming to conclusions about impacts and actions. They can be an important source of comfort to each other as they sort the likely consequences of an event within the whole range of imagined consequences.

Thoughts about a Combination of a Person with an Intuitive Preference Joined to a Person with a Sensor Preference in Marriage

This is a challenging combination. Again, this is a combination that I know well. Frances and I have lived with this for forty-six years. In our marriage, and other couples we know with this contrast, we see the challenges. The person with the intuitive preference may see an event, like an overdue bill or note from a child's teacher, as a much deeper matter than it actually is. When the sensor preference spouse does not seem deeply concerned, it can frustrate the intuitive preference spouse. After a while, the spouse with the intuitive preference can end up bearing much of the worry alone. It can be a hard life as a person with intuitive preference in a sensor preference world. Likewise it can be hard for a person with a sensor preference living with a spouse who has an intuitive preference. The person with the intuitive preference can overreact to even simple events or statements. The intuitive preference spouse can be slow to convey information, and when it comes, it may be cluttered with add-on extrapolations and interpretations. The person with the intuitive preference can be hurt by things intended to be merely information rather than big events.

Whether it is in the workplace or marriage, occasionally the extrapolations of the intuitive preference are on target and the directness of the sensor preference useful. A couple can gain strength by knowing the personality preference difference that the S preference spouse and N preference spouse bring to the marriage. The intuitive preference can open the door to things that could affect the marriage in many ways. The person with the intuitive preference can be the safety valve on the family budget or parenting matters to guide the couple on a healthy long-term course. This spouse can see and surface risks that are not obvious. This spouse can spot some of the cautionary things a couple should consider pertaining to risky things. In return, the spouse with the sensor preference provides stability and reality. This spouse can lead the couple as they sift through the spectrum of worries. In our marriage, we probably would not be living part of our year in Hawai'i without my intuitive preference imagination combined with Frances's practical sensor preference view confirming that we could really do it.

JIM KRUPKA

Thinker (T) Preference versus Feeler (F) Preference: Primary Basis for Our Decisions: Logic versus Emotion

Like the S/N contrast, this element of personality type has a big impact on how we experience our relationship. It is big because of its impact on how we use the information we gather to reach a decision. We all use some kind of process inside us to get to decisions. An individual with a thinker preference compared to an individual with a feeler preference will use the same information but follow a different path to an answer. Here I am not talking about speed of decision. Some people are proud of being able to act quickly on the "gut" while others pride themselves in deep deliberation. Whether a person moves quickly or deliberates at length, both use some platform based on the T/F spectrum to make decisions.

The person with the thinker preference will depend on logic. They can take things literally and convey things with clarity. They can seem very logical in all types of situations. They can be known as cool and calm when things get tough. A key characteristic is their tendency to decide toward what is fair—not necessarily what makes people happy. The person with a thinker preference likes to prove points logically. The observer can hear the path of logic spill out in their words. Their strength is being objective as they make tough decisions. They have a bit of thick skin and can make decisions knowing that it is better to be right than popular. From these observations, it is evident how useful someone with this thinker personality preference is in marriage.

People with a feeler preference are more dependent on emotion as they make decisions. A person with a feeler preference knows that good decisions need to take people into account. They will work extra hard to satisfy people's needs. Often their words show how they can identify with other people and imagine life in other people's shoes. Harmony matters a lot—even more than clarity. In working with others, a person with a feeler preference can be frustrated while wondering if others really care.

A scriptural story to demonstrate this difference comes from a contrast of the Law of Moses to the Gospel of Jesus. God knew he had created thinking people, so he told them in Deuteronomy 5:7, "You shall not have other gods beside me." Deuteronomy 5:11 says, "You shall not invoke the name of the LORD, your God, in vain." And so on. Everything a person with a thinker preference needs to hear to function is included in this covenant with God.

In Matthew 22:37–40, Jesus delivers a similar template for life, but with a style like a feeler.

> He said to him, "You shall love the Lord, your God, with all your heart, with all your soul, and with all your mind. This is the greatest and the first commandment. The second is like it: You shall love your neighbor as yourself. The whole law and the prophets depend on these two commandments."

Jesus seems to use a style that would be very comfortable for someone with a feeler preference. He wraps up the essence of the Ten Commandments into a summary with feeling.

Looking at the makeup of society, most men have a thinker preference and most women have a feeler preference. These are accepted norms. For a man or woman to excel with the opposite preference is a challenge. Also, it is important to remember every person has some amount of the opposite preference. None of the contrasts are so extreme in someone that they completely lack some amount of the contrasting preference. The preferences are not absolute. People who have a preference as a thinker still feel. Likewise people who have a feeler preference still think.

In marriage, we depend on a combination of emotion and logic to guide our lives. It is overly simple to accept the T/F contrast as represented in the popular 1950s sitcom formula of emotional, irrational wife and logical, unfeeling husband. That is not generally how I see it in couples. The world is filled with much more variety. Knowing the T/F preference of each spouse can aid in understanding how things are experienced in the marriage.

So like the other contrasts, the following are some comments based on observations of personality preference impacts in couples I have worked with.

Thoughts for Two Thinker Preference People Joined in Marriage

The good news is both have a similar lens to filter information as they receive it. Both tend to take things logically. Being alike on this personality driver means less stress than if they had a contrast. Like the S/N contrast, both should be comfortable communicating what they are experiencing and what they believe should happen. When they see the same things, they usually can guide each other to understand how each sees things. This allows tangible actions to deal with tangible events. The risk is that some human implications of the events may escape this couple since both are generally logical. This couple will not be known as people who *wear their feelings on their sleeve.* They will have strength in neighborhood poker games. Others, like their children or neighbors in the community, might see things with more emotion and judge this couple as unfeeling or cold. In this couple, it would be handy to develop a habit of asking each other how the other feels about things since feelings may not spill out naturally. This would be especially useful when they have children. In families, emotions matter, and logic alone is not enough to make family life as joy filled as it could be.

Thoughts about Two People with a Feeler Preference Joined in Marriage

The good news is that this couple will not have much trouble knowing when something is upsetting. Emotion will be very visible. Even if they both have a clear introvert preference, facial expressions and actions will deliver messages. Stress can come since each is easily hurt. Even innocent comments can deliver an emotional hurt that was not intended. Like the S/N contrast, one or the other may be thinking too hard about the impact of the news on the other. There will be perception of how the other feels. At times, this can inhibit communication since one or the other hesitates to say what needs to be said to avoid hurting their spouse. This couple needs good communication skills to facilitate constructive dialogue aimed at putting things in proper perspective and logically coming to conclusions about impacts and actions. They do not have to worry about taking the human factors into consideration. They are good at that. They may need to put important deliberations down on paper or find some other way to force logic into an emotional process. It would be handy for this couple to get into a habit of recognizing when emotion is driving an important decision and have one or the other say, "Hey, wait a minute. Let's think about this."

Thoughts about a Person with a Feeler Preference Joined in Marriage to Someone with a Thinker Preference

This contrast can be challenging. The same words or actions that seem sensible to the one with the thinker preference can gnaw deep inside their spouse with a feeler preference. In our marriage, the difference often surfaces in how an experience feels. If someone says something at a party that has a hint of criticism, I, the person with the feeler preference, take the comment internally and experience emotion that can spoil the experience. When Frances detects that I am upset by something someone says, she is good at bringing me back to a balanced, logical perspective. She will remind me about the context of the comment, who said it, and how it fit with everything else that may have gone on that evening. This combination can be strong if they use type language to appreciate the view of each other. When making big decisions, both preferences bring strengths to the table. This couple is lucky enough to have both preferences present when needed. The trick is to understand how both preferences are viewing an issue and draw on those different views to make a decision.

In our marriage, this contrast of personality preference has led at times to emotional hurt for me that really had no reason to be there. For Frances, there has been frustration over emotional reactions from me that, in the context of everything else, had no reason to be there. In our conversations, I may tell Frances something that I am excited about. For example, just the other day, I found something in our grocery store that we had been looking for for months. I was excited and felt the emotion. Not a big deal but my expectations were that Frances would express similar joy at my find. Instead, without reaction, she went on with her shopping. To her, I had produced the logical result of repeatedly looking for the item in the store. Other times she will tell me something that was just a statement of fact like "Glad we got that done" after a long day working on a project. If I have been emotionally involved in the project and engaged with energy, this comment can be a letdown or—worse—a worry. Feeling what I detect as disappointment on something that was a big deal for me, I respond with questions about how she felt about what we did and whether she really wanted to do it. With my emotion, she has to respond to something that for her was no big issue.

The person with a feeler preference will feel overly concerned or criticized on things that seem trivial to the person with a thinker preference. The person with the thinker preference will feel frustrated about an overly emotional reaction to something that really did not seem worth much emotion. This contrast is serious since it affects how we feel about things and how we feel about how our spouse is acting. It will also affect our decisions since this T/F element of personality preference is what we use to make decisions.

Also, in marriage, how we feel about things affects how we feel about the marriage. Most of the situations we face are ordinary and, in the scheme of life, no big deal. But when these logic/emotional T/F differences of preference accumulate, discontent can mount. For Frances and me, the key to getting through these differences with less lingering emotion is to understand our T/F personality preference difference.

Like the S/N contrast, despite the stresses that come from difference in the T/F preferences, there is gain. The person with the feeler preference is easy to read. The person with the feeler preference will help guide the couple through the human side of family and social relationships. Someone married to a person with a feeler preference will have no problem knowing when their spouse is happy or disappointed. The person with the thinker preference is levelheaded and a stabilizing force in a marriage. During times of stress, this is a very handy preference to have in a marriage. Someone married to a person with a thinker preference will have no problem keeping things in context. The thinker preference spouse can guide the couple toward solutions to problems that get lost in the emotion of the spouse with the feeler preference.

Any of these personality preferences can work in marriage. The road to joy comes from understanding each other's preferences and drawing from the best of each as a couple. Contrasts like this one really show the beauty of the divine plan of marriage. The two become one and are far better than each alone.

Judging (J) Preference versus Perceiving (P) Preference: How We Build Our Path of Life

The last personality preference contrast is the J/P, which is judging versus perceiving. As we all take in information, we eventually have to do something with it. This personality preference contrast addresses our path toward action. This letter contrast of preferences is a clue to whether our mental processes are driven by how we process information, the S/N processes, or how we make decisions, the T/F processes.

For the person with a judger preference, everything has a place. As they look at information before them, often the answer to a problem or opportunity is obvious. The judger preference directs the mental process to making a decision. Because they know what is right and know that others are looking at the same information, the other person, spouse for example, should get the same answer with the same clarity. In the church, we are good at judging. I was asked to facilitate a team-building session for two parishes being clustered under a single pastor. The marriage of parishes was not going smoothly. In response to this request, I arranged for each of the twenty-two people who were part of the parish leadership teams to take the MBTI. Of the twenty-two people, twenty-one had a J preference. Over the last four years, I have kept a tally of personality preferences for our marriage preparation couples. In that four-year collection of over one hundred people, people with a judger preference are also in the majority.

The person with a judger preference is good to have around and often is good as a leader. They know that if only people would do what they should, things would be fine. So their job is to help others see that. They are efficient with organization, often having a plan for each day. They keep lists and use them. They likely maintain order in work space and home. Because they see things clearly, they can be frustrated when others do not. Depending on their other personality preferences, their frustration can become visible. They can be accused of being angry even when they are just stating facts. In the end, since they know what is right, priority 1 is to get to it and get things done.

A person with a P, perceiver preference, is exciting to be around. They can see many possibilities. Nothing is necessarily an open-and-shut case. I picture perceivers sometimes as human bubble machines continually bringing something new. Since they have so much thought generation going on, they can be easily distracted by new ideas. Part of the adventure comes from appetite to explore the unknown. Because they may be mentally tracking so many ideas, they may need some last-minute spurts to get things done. In their workplace or home, neatness may not the greatest factor. A person with a perceiver preference can also make most work fun and handle a variety of projects moving from subject to subject. This is not the kind of person who is quick to commit to a decision. You may hear reactions like "Don't pin me down!"

My scriptural example for this contrast comes from Genesis 18, the story of Sodom and Gomorrah. God had enough of Sodom and Gomorrah. The judging side of God speaks.

> So the LORD said: The outcry against Sodom and Gomorrah is so great, and their sin so grave, that I must go down to see whether or not their actions are as bad as the cry against them that comes to me. I mean to find out. (Genesis 18:20–21)

But the perceiving Abraham does not see the case as closed at all. Genesis 18:23–25 says,

Then Abraham drew near and said: "Will you really sweep away the righteous with the wicked? Suppose there were fifty righteous people in the city; would you really sweep away and not spare the place for the sake of the fifty righteous people within it? Far be it from you to do such a thing, to kill the righteous with the wicked, so that the righteous and the wicked are treated alike! Far be it from you! Should not the judge of all the world do what is just?"

In the end, we see the strength of both. God did not rush to judgment. Rather he gave the two cities every possible chance in response to Abraham's vision of possibilities. However, God's initial judgment is right, and the cities were destroyed.

This is a powerful divider of types. In society overall, people with a judger preference are in a slight majority. Along with the S/N divide, the J/P divide can say much about how an individual will behave. While the S/N contrast describes how information is taken in and initially used, the J/P type describes what we do or the decisions we make from that information. People with a J preference can directly get to decisions and are frustrated when others can't get there. People with a P preference are always looking at possibilities to the frustration of others who have enough information to make a decision.

In marriage and families, decisions have to be made. As two become one, the two can recognize the decision-making style of each other and become stronger. Part of this is recognizing the decision-making style of the families of origin. In your marriage, bring in what you know about the decision-making style in the home you grew up in. Add an understanding of the J/P personality preference of you and your spouse to find your own strong style.

So like the other contrasts, the following are some comments based on observations of J/P personality preference in couples I experienced.

Thoughts for Two People with a Judger Preference Joined in Marriage

This couple will have a strong sense of values and know what is right. The challenge can be if there are differences in their basic values due to background and experiences. It is good for the couple to talk about why they are making a specific decision to expose underlying assumptions. This is especially important in the romance phase when differences will not automatically surface. Once two people with a judger preference come to terms on basic values, they will find decision-making pretty easy. One loss in that process is the potential for new and exciting experiences that are outside their core experience. Things like "Where shall we go for our vacation?" may seem open-and-shut based on experience. But there may be new ideas that could really enhance the marriage.

For two judgers, finding new things outside of the status quo is hard but can yield good fruit when discovery happens. This is something Frances and I discovered. About thirteen years into our marriage, I proposed a move beyond our usual vacations camping or visiting family to include a Caribbean resort vacation. It was a stretch on our budget and a challenge with five young kids. I could feel the judgment of others given my imaginations about their impression of us as neglectful parents. But we did it with planning and a grandparent visit. That trip was a life changer in the way it energized our marriage. We had not been away as a couple for a decade and had no idea how much we needed to do it. More recently our decision to add a second home and ministry in Hawai'i came to be when Frances opened a door to that possibility. Before that, I assumed that such a change was completely out of bounds for us because of Frances's desire for stability. Now five years into that, we are so glad she opened that door. But that door opening was not natural for a couple of clear J preference people.

Thoughts about Two People with a Perceiver Preference Joined in Marriage

Such a household must really be exciting. With husband and wife both natural idea and opportunity generators, there should be no shortage of sources of adventure. The challenge can be focus and closure. This couple might benefit from some disciplined goal setting that can provide a general roadmap to follow. They also will need to encourage each other to come to a decision in a timely manner. They may frustrate their children or friends as decisions linger while the two perceiver preference spouses remain engaged in looking at new possibilities. As such, they need to think about expectations of those who depend on them for decisions and find some middle ground on timeliness of the decision.

Thoughts about a Perceiver Preference Person with a Judger Preference Spouse

This contrast can be a big win or burden for a couple depending on how aware they are of the differences between them and how communication and negotiation happens in their marriage. With good understanding of each other's preferences and good communication, the result is life to its fullest. Without that understanding and communication, frustration will be big for both.

The person with the perceiver preference can bring some exciting ideas that the person with the judger preference just will not see. Ideas could cover everything from home style to vacations and the bedroom. The person with the perceiver preference will need to be aware of the boundaries of the person with the judger preference and present new ideas in the context of those boundaries. This does not mean that things outside the boundaries will not find a place in this marriage. They might, and it could be very exciting. The process just needs to bring the idea into a comfort zone for the person who has a judger preference. When the person with a judger preference is aware of the potential for new things from the person with the perceiver preference and the perceiver preference spouse is aware of the judger preference spouse's comfort zone, great things can happen.

Wrapping up this discussion of MBTI preferences, do you have an idea of what your personality preferred type is? What about your spouse? Spend some time talking together about your similarities and differences. Talk about the impact these contrasts have on your marriage. At the end of this chapter is an abbreviated list describing some impacts of personality preferences in marriage to help you in this discussion. Things like communication, finance, sex, faith, arguing, and parenting are experienced differently depending on personality preference. Awareness of the differences can be powerful in strengthening a marriage.

A Shortcut to Understanding Personality Preferences

David Keirsey and Marilyn Bates, in their book *Please Understand Me,* used two components of the MBTI as a shortcut.[21] The Myers & Briggs Foundation refers to the same combinations as "Function Pairs."[22] Keirsey and Bates called the combination of the two "temperament." They combined the MBTI type preferences describing how we gather information—"trees" vs. "forest" indicated by S/N preference—and how we use information indicated by T/F type preference. Their methodology ends up with four combinations that they identified as

- rational: NT
- idealist: NF
- artisan: SP
- guardian: SJ

The following descriptions provide a few points to consider about characteristics and preferences of each of the four temperaments. The comments are generic and applicable to any situation. But here, think about the temperaments in terms of your marriage. Words that describe feelings or comforts apply so much more to marriage than any other situation. Since in marriage, we are talking about enduring covenants that mean "no leaving" when things are not right, it is important to understand your temperament and that of your spouse. You need to find ways to enrich your lives respectful of who you are.

---

[21] Wikipedia, "Please Understand Me," https://en.wikipedia.org/wiki/Please_Understand_Me, last edited July 25, 2019
[22] Myers & Briggs Foundation, "MBTI Certification Program Participant's Resource Guide," 2018, page 27

As you consider my comments on each of these temperaments, think of what it is like to have a person with that particular temperament as a partner in marriage. If it is you, how closely do these words describe you? More importantly, how do they help explain how you feel about your marriage or what you want in your marriage? Similarly, what is your spouse's temperament? How do these words fit him or her? How does this identification of temperament help you understand how he or she acts? Also, how does this explain his or her happiness or stress?

The NF Temperament

This is a temperament that loves people. They also are people recognized for extraordinary social acts. They can be idealists and known as do-gooders. Part of this comes from their deep emotional involvement combined with intuitive imagination of possibilities. When engaged in a cause, or in a marriage, they are full in. They personalize everything.

NF strengths include a great capacity for working with others; they draw other people out. They can be articulate and persuasive even as people with an introvert preference. They have a strong desire to help others. They make very loving and devoted spouses.

The NF temperament brings potential challenges. It is hard to disagree with an NF spouse. Their arguments can be well thought out considering a range of implications and are communicated with emotion. However, there can also be times when emotion will explode if that trust is violated, particularly in an extravert preference spouse. An introvert preference spouse may withdraw if that same trust is violated.

The NT Temperament

They make good planners and researchers. They seem to be always asking why. They can be driven to excellence and be adventure and risk takers. The intuitive and logical combination gives them the gift to see the big picture. They can be good at conceptualizing and planning. This is the spouse to plan the vacation or work on the retirement plan. With careful exploration of possibilities, they can bring a marriage and family to amazing levels of excellence.

The challenge for an NT comes from his or her logical assessment of people and things around them, which gives them an amazing level of internal confidence. With logic prevailing over emotion, their attachment to someone lasts as long as it is logically sound. In a marriage grounded in covenant, the marriage will last, but there will be off and on moments depending on how things are going at the time. The judging process continues with initial acceptance, but that is just the start of further evaluation. The non-NT spouse may have less tolerance for this ongoing critique than the NT. Since they can always see logical possibilities, the status quo is difficult, which can challenge a non-NT spouse who sees things as fine as they are.

The SJ Temperament

This group makes up a large part of our population. They are the organization people we see carrying on with what is "right." Things as basic as motherhood and organized religion with Boy Scout values make this group popular and effective leaders. They make good CEOs and hold more of those positions than any other temperament. They are in their comfort zone with traditional ways in everything from reading instructions to making love. Because they combine ability to sense situations and judge what is right, they are comfortable stepping up as great organizers and build a good track record doing it.

This group has obvious strengths that serve society and marriages well. They are strong administrators. They are dependable and can take charge. When not in charge, they honor and follow the leader. They do not judge the leader or worry when a leader is ineffective since they know the system will prevail over individual incompetence.

There are some challenges for SJs. One of the biggest is being married to another SJ. There is not always room for two people who want to be boss.

They also can miss opportunities that would enhance a marriage by relying on what they sense to be right. They also can miss evolutionary change. Times can change before our eyes, and an SJ may not always see it. In recent decades, many institutions have suffered from this as organizations continue blindly under outmoded business models. Eastman Kodak, the maker of camera film, just did not see the digital age fast enough. The SJ has less patience for people than institutions. So if the non-SJ spouse is trying to bring something new to a marriage, an SJ may be slow to engage and may be uncomfortable when pushed to something new. On the other hand, they are able to patiently wait for change when it seems right and eventually get on a new course when it is right. The non-SJ spouse needs to have patience. The SJ will at some point come around to something that evidence shows will add to the marriage.

The SP Temperament

This person can be practical, drawing from his or her preference as a sensor. They can be creative problem solvers based on their wide field of vision as perceivers. Things are always open. They are not as ready to look at everything as open-and-shut as someone with a judger preference. They also can have a sense of the immediate that can be productive taking advantage of opportunities on the spot. Challenges can come from fast action that can create a crisis since judgment is not always in the forefront. To the contrary, they can keep many decisions open while options are explored to the frustration of others. Their spouse or family can wonder, *Are you ever going to decide?*

An SP preferring spouse can bring adventure to a marriage by finding new things to do and experience. They can be idea generators when challenges with kids or other family issues are at hand. They can be quick to pick up signals that something needs attention and immediately begin to think of solutions. The sensor preference brings substance and reality to their many ideas.

The challenges for someone married to an SP preferring spouse can be an appearance of being *now* focused versus the long term. This spouse may want a new boat to create more family time in the summer. But this action can worry a NT or NF preferring spouse who is thinking about college bills and retirement. The sensor preference component of the SP can also frustrate a spouse with a feeler preference by missing some of the emotion that is important to a feeler. The feeler may have a need to get out of the house on a date while the sensor just does not see the need, saying, "We had a date last week."

Putting All of This Personality Preference Knowledge to Work

It is important to remember that we all have some element of each preference within us. Also, every combination of personality preferences and types can work in marriage. Some combinations are harder than others. A marriage with no person having an extravert preference to start conversations can be challenging. A marriage of S/N preference contrasts, T/F contrasts, or J/P contrasts has its challenges. If multiple contrasts exist, the challenge is magnified.

The key to making it in marriage despite the contrasts is the covenant commitment to remain married. With that commitment, a couple can find ways to understand and work through any contrast of preferences. Frances and I are living examples of a long-married couple with serious personality preference contrasts. As two people with introvert and judger preferences complicated by S/N and T/F preference contrasts, we have challenges. But we both entered marriage with an absolute covenant commitment. That is the solid foundation that allows us to work through the challenges that come out of our different preferences. Understanding our personality preferences has been the single greatest leap in the comfort and joy of our marriage.

Understanding of differences turns the differences into an advantage that can enrich a marriage. For you, understanding each other's personality preference is more than just a way to survive marriage. It is a powerful path to increase joy in life and marriage. This understanding enhances communication in both giving and receiving information. This understanding more importantly brings an awareness of how events, words, and actions are internalized by each person. This understanding is core to being better at important dimensions of living a life together. This understanding leads to better management of marital finances and problem solving. It also enriches life in things as diverse as leisure activities and sex. Indeed, with understanding of personality type, two become one and are better for it.

Type Implications for Important Dimensions of Marriage

The list that follows is a tool to help you consider how you might be experiencing important parts of married life far differently than your spouse. It is vitally important to understand the personality type preference differences of husband and wife to gain joy out of the differences rather than frustration. The list is far from complete but worth thinking about as a couple. It is intended to provide some food for thought to help you understand how personality preferences affect your lives in marriage.

Communication

- Introvert: Thoughtful and reserved. Needs time to think. Can be slow to respond. Can be perceived as uninterested based on no immediate response, but when responses (or statements) come, they are well thought out.
- Extravert: Spontaneous and free flowing. Can seem incomplete and scattered. Can overwhelm an introvert, but there is no mystery about what is in his or her head because it is all spoken.
- Sensor: What is observed is said. Can be very focused, missing broader implications.
- Intuitive: What is implied by observations is only the beginning. May respond beyond the issue. Hears basic facts but translates on the fly to a bigger picture.
- Thinker: Logical in making a point. Confident that their message will land as wanted because it makes sense. May miss some of the intangible human elements that reside in feelings.

- Feeler: Feeling can be detected in words chosen. Feelings may detract from effective communication by missing logical points as emotion erodes listening. May be hurt by words designed merely to convey a benign fact.
- Judger: Well-meaning but closed and decisive. Can come off strong since "right" should prevail. Very direct in words along the experience-based proper path. Frustrated by someone who is not focused.
- Perceiver: Open to possibilities. May drift in several directions since all is possible. Needs to hear ideas and frustrated when being told, "This is how it has always been, and this is how it is."

Finances

- Introvert: Deliberated internally. Ideas and worries may not naturally flow. When expressed, are very solid thoughts.
- Extravert: Talked out before fully considered. Will share ideas and worries even as they form. Expressing thoughts is a part of forming a sound direction.
- Sensor: As sensed by conditions of the day. Realistic to degree that current state is realistic. May have a tendency to make financial decisions based on the financial situation at the time: I have the money, so I'll buy it.
- Intuitive: Long-range implications matter. Imagines things good and bad growing from today. Big picture. May be conservative on buying today, worried about tomorrow.
- Thinker: Fact based. Probably backed up by analysis. Plans formed with goal in mind.
- Feeler: Emotion, fears, and excitement. Could lead to splurges or missing the spice of life. Strongest when able to balance worry and impulse.
- Judger: A right way to do it. Likes a set of values and rules. May be self-defined rules like a budget or attitude toward use of credit.
- Perceiver: Within reason, unlimited potential. Let's explore. React at last minute. Less confined by set ways of spending and saving. Will need a means of financial discipline.

Sex

- Introvert: Difficult to verbalize wants and wishes.
- Extravert: Comfort verbalizing anything. Thrive on giving and receiving feedback.
- Sensor: Day by day as life unfolds. If it was good last time, it will be good next time. Don't break it if it works.
- Intuitive: Even if it's good today, there could be more. Worry about being good enough, and fantasize seeking more.
- Thinker: A leads to B. Sex manuals have a place. Preplanned romance.
- Feeler: Feelings directed toward other and self. Worry about satisfying partner while fantasizing about more. Can be attracted to a romance novel life.
- Judger: Within accepted norms of couple, church, and society. Uncomfortable pushing edges.
- Perceiver: Many things are possible within wide boundaries. Let's have some fun!

Faith

- Introvert: Internal prayer and discernment. More deliberate thought than spontaneous.
- Extravert: Verbalized, comfort with others in prayer. Enjoy external energy in prayer. Can be very spontaneous.
- Sensor: What is, is. Tradition is important. Expects faith and reality of life to align.
- Intuitive: The infinite is vast, and paths may lead in many directions. Life today is only the beginning.
- Thinker: Since I believe this, I then can believe that. Apologetics is powerful.
- Feeler: Faith happens inside. Conversion of the heart more than the head.
- Judger: Organized religion is good. Provides boundaries. No need to figure it out alone.

- Perceiver: The universe is vast and a mystery. Doctrine is a starting point.

Arguing

- Introvert: Hesitant to start. Need time to respond. Pent-up issue can explode. Can be disadvantaged in conflict.
- Extravert: Words flow. Responses can form quickly. May start an argument without intent. Can be advantaged in conflict.
- Sensor: Things seem clear, supporting strong arguments. Can be inflexible. Can be puzzled that spouse could see things differently. "What's wrong with you?"
- Intuitive: Things can be more than meet the eye. May go in directions a sensor cannot imagine. Can be puzzled by spouse's inflexibility.
- Thinker: Logic prevails. Hard to understand how someone could see things differently. Puzzled by an emotional response to a rational issue.
- Feeler: Emotions prevail. Just sticking to the facts neglects importance of people. Can be very convincing.
- Judger: What is right is clear. Not much room to go beyond established boundaries. Seems rigid. May be predictable.
- Perceiver: There is not necessarily one right answer. Not good when confined. May wander into new turf just because he or she can.

Parenting

- Introvert: Deeply thinks about difficult issues before raising them. Thinks then speaks.
- Extravert: Communicates often and on anything. Listening can be a challenge. May say or allow things off the cuff that he or she may later regret.
- Sensor: In touch with children to degree that actions and evidence show. May miss emotions. Can be permissive if things look in good shape when a little more engagement might be warranted.

- Intuitive: Takes actions and goes beyond. Intuition may lead to too much worry or too much comfort. Can be a very involved parent.
- Thinker: Parenting books and authority have a place. Good as long as kids follow the book.
- Feeler: Deep emotional engagement. Feels discipline more than kids. May exaggerate things unnecessarily.
- Judger: There is right and wrong. Tough love at times. May not appreciate emotions to the level kids feel.
- Perceiver: There is not always a clear right and wrong. May give kids too much space.

Chapter 7

MONEY AND FINANCES: A MARRIAGE MAKER OR BREAKER

The saying goes something like "Money can't buy happiness, but it sure helps." In looking at marriages around us, this is true. Scriptures are filled with words about the blessings of poverty, and the church calls us to a preferential option for the poor. In Matthew 6:24–29, we are taught about money in relation to our spiritual life.

> No one can serve two masters. He will either hate one and love the other, or be devoted to one and despise the other. You cannot serve God and mammon. "Therefore I tell you, do not worry about your life, what you will eat [or drink], or about your body, what you will wear. Is not life more than food and the body more than clothing? Look at the birds in the sky; they do not sow or reap, they gather nothing into barns, yet your heavenly Father feeds them. Are not you more important than they? Can any of you by worrying add a single moment to your life-span? Why are you anxious about clothes? Learn from the way the wild flowers grow. They do not work or spin. But I tell you that not even Solomon in all his splendor was clothed like one of them.

Those are wonderful words core to putting money and things in perspective. But we still need to eat, have a place to live, and care for our family. In our society, that takes money. We are all in different situations. We come from different families with different resources. We have different employment gifts and opportunities. These differences drive big differences in our need for and ability to get money to live. I already mentioned the couple that helps us with marriage preparation who seem to have a very joy-filled life raising six children with little wealth. They witness to tremendous faith in the words expressed in Matthew's Gospel. From another perspective, a priest friend I admire for his ability to connect with people privately commented about his life as a priest compared to his congregation. He said,

> I am so humbled looking out at the people in this church. When I think about all they have to worry about … feeding their families, paying bills, taking care of households, I am overwhelmed. I don't have to worry about any of that.

The contrast between the priest and many of his people shows the practical challenge of putting money in its proper place in marriage. Every household is different. In some, many things are taken care of outside the immediate family's need to make money. In other families, they are on their own to meet every bit of the practical needs of life. That means money is important. The questions are these: how much is really needed, and how do we manage money to keep the spiritual side of life at the forefront?

I once gave a homily on the scripture story of the rich man and his chances of getting to heaven. You will remember that story says that the man's chances are lower than that of a camel passing through a needle's eye. The theme I tried to express is that money in itself is not evil. Jesus had rich friends and depended on them for hospitality and life's needs as he traveled. But he was never attached to money. He was like my priest friend who is able to take what God provides and be satisfied with that. In my homily that was directed to a parish with some people of wealth, the challenge I delivered was for each to come to terms with knowing when enough is enough. That is a critical thing to sort out in marriage through a combination of budgeting, planning, goal setting, and prayer.

JIM KRUPKA

Unity: Money in a Covenant Marriage: Impact on Marriage Stability

Issues rooted in money are the second highest cause of divorce, right behind infidelity.[23] In couples that I have been with having money-driven marriage strife, the cause is usually not about having enough money. I have not encountered any couple whose marriage was in trouble because of lack of money. Everyone I worked with had issues deeper than money. The biggest issue is lack of communication and subsequent lack of unity. When it comes to money, usually one spouse initiated some financial action without involving the other. Often the financial action was taken to cover for another problem. In one case, a wife borrowed and stole to cover a drug problem. Another was trying to deal with financial challenges and got taken in by an easy money scam. A husband added a large amount of debt to cover bills and did not tell his wife until the debt mountain got big. In each of these, the spouse who caused the big problem was making some attempt to deal with a problem that did not start terribly big. The difficulty came because the one spouse was acting alone. The other had no idea what was happening until things were way out of hand. In defense of the spouses who caused the problems, they believed that they could work their way out. The hope was to fix the embarrassing problem before their spouses found out. As bad as these cases sound, to my knowledge, all of these couples are still married.

Unity in money and finance is not hard for the couple that wants to do it. The key is to start building a platform of unity before the wedding. Begin by complete openness with your spouse-to-be about debts and obligations. This can be a test of love and unity from the start. If you have a large amount of credit card debt and your fiancé has been as frugal as can be, it is embarrassing to lay that out. It will feel like a risk to expose that picture. It is hard when you open up something you are embarrassed about to the one you want to love you when you know that some of your past actions may not be very lovable. Doing this can be a great step in building a covenant marriage because it brings the strength of you as a couple to solve a problem that is harder to solve alone. Establishing this pattern of

---

[23] Shellie Warren, *"10 Most Common Reasons for Divorce,"* Marriage.com, https://www.marriage.com/advice/divorce/10-most-common-reasons-for-divorce/, 2019

honesty early will give you strength later on dealing with things beyond money. This is getting naked without shame in a much more courageous way than taking off your clothes. If you are forming a covenant marriage, this financial nakedness happens with love, not shame.

From our own experience and experiences of other long-married couples, sharing everything financially is important. This means combining accounts, living off of a joint checking account, and paying bills together. Frances and I have done this from the beginning, and it has paid off. We settled early on sharing the financial chores in a way that even a double-entry accountant could love. We prepare a detailed budget together. The month we were married, we combined all finances into a single joint account. When we started a family and Frances stayed home, she wrote the checks and paid the bills. I tracked income and spending in a detailed budget spreadsheet. This way, we both saw every bit of income and spending that we had. That made unity possible since nothing was hidden and each part of that spending got there through some thought from both of us. That has taken a lot of the money stress off us as a couple because when we have a challenge, we both see it and are together in finding a solution.

It also has been a formula to make some amazing dreams come true through unified financial stewardship. We left the corporate world and started a dream business, our farm and vineyard, in our early fifties. We were able to do mission work at considerable cost of time and money possible because we planned for it. We put five kids through college. We are well beyond a tithe in charitable sharing. This all happened because we were together in working through financial challenges from the day we were married. While money is not the source of joy for us, it certainly reduces the worry. Financial unity is a big part of magnifying joy in marriage.

When we talk about financial unity and complete merging of accounts, we often get asked about the need for a little "whim" money held in a personal account. It is an interesting question because it shows a little residual nervousness on the part of the woman or man about losing all opportunity to satisfy a personal want. "What if I want to buy some clothes or do something with my girlfriends?" We do not fight the idea but do not encourage it either. In our joint budget, we have a whim category that lets us enjoy some luxury purchases. We also have a gift budget that includes gifts for each other. That may not sound romantic, but it does enhance romance because it removes the worry of one spending much more than the other on presents. Also, as far as personal spending, we do get to enjoy some personal whims but almost always after consulting with the other before we spend. If I want to go to a game with a friend, I talk it over with Frances before doing it. If she wants to go to an art show, she does the same with me. I cannot remember a time when one of us has vetoed the other on a personal wish. There have not been vetoes because we have a budget and are not selfish in how we approach spending it. This is key to covenant love and unity. We use even this whim piece of our budget as a tool for giving to the other rather than a tool to see how much we individually can get.

Do Not Overspend on the Wedding: Do Not Borrow for a Party!

A step in starting financial life together on good footing is to avoid overspending on the wedding. The most important thing on your wedding day is cementing the covenant of love in your hearts. That commitment is not at all affected by any glamour or party on your wedding day. As a clergyman, it is sad to see a bride or mother of a bride stressed to the point that they miss the joy of the day because of details of the wedding. There is worry about photographers or caterers doing what they are supposed to do and so on. In our family, both of our married children had modest weddings. They made extensive use of friends for music, food, and photography. One of our daughters fed her wedding guests Popeyes fried chicken with potluck sides from friends. I heard one of the guests comment, "We go to weddings all the time. We eat wedding food then go out to Popeye's for what we really want. Here we got what we like right at the wedding!" Our other daughter spent modestly on a very nice wedding then used what they saved for a coast-to-coast, eighty-day bicycle trip.

A wedding-related financial and relationship problem I increasingly see is the destination wedding. These are weddings in some nice resort location.

The weddings are usually small with just a few friends and family. They are justified as providing a very nice experience for close friends and family without the cost and organization of a big wedding at home. This is bad logic from many angles. First, this puts an expensive burden on the guests who come. Our adult daughters tell us that they are stressed by pressure to participate in some of these. They really do not get to enjoy the resort because they are wrapped into the obligations related to the wedding. It robs them of vacation time and money that could be enjoyed more on something fitting their tastes and personal life.

I cannot say it enough: keep your wedding simple and on a modest budget. Definitely do not borrow for the wedding. Find a way to have a very good day with family and friends within the resources that you have. It is the making the covenant that counts, not the party.

Spending with Compass: Make a Budget, and Stick to It

It is amazing how much little things add up. For example, a $4 latte every workday morning adds up to about $1,000 a year. Buying lunch instead of bringing a brown bag from home is $1,500 or more a year. If two of you do that, that's $5,000 after taxes from your income every year. This type of spending is an invisible budget killer. It seems so small yet really is big.

We were frugal when we got married largely because we grew up in rural, nonaffluent families. Brown bagging, instant coffee, and eating leftovers were normal parts of working life. Best of all, we both grew up feeling rich. We began with a budget formed jointly, but it did not feel tight. Coming out of college, Fran's $6,000 per year teaching job and my engineering job brought in more money than we ever imagined. After a year of marriage, my job was moved from Oklahoma to Colorado, which brought at least a temporary end to our second income. Things got tighter, and we had to be more careful. However, we still had a margin of error. Over the next five years, we added three kids and started to think about our future life more. It was at that stage that we began watching every penny. Frances started her budget tracking book that continued for years. I reported even ten-cent cups of coffee. What I remember most about that experience was the degree of unity that budget and tracking system gave us. What was less obvious was that that was the time when our financial health took a lasting step forward.

Building a budget as a couple is a must. Be sure and prepare it to a level of detail that will give it strength. This is not a money management book, so I will not go deeper on this topic other than to offer some resources and say again, "Do it!" There are many tools to help you do this. Good marriage preparation programs like the one we use include workbook pages to guide you through it. Financial companies have free online budget tools that guide you through short- and long-term budget preparation. One resource that has been helpful for many couples and is even used formally by some church marriage preparation programs comes from author Dave Ramsey. His books and lectures on money are excellent.

Importance of Being in It Together, Drawing on Every Tool You Have

The budgeting templates provide a good and tangible start to force communication and partnership in the money part of marriage. In the process, it is important to draw from all the tools you have. Some of the tools come from your family of origin. Talk about how money was managed in the family you came from. What problems and blessings were apparent? Also draw from what you know about each other. Use tools like the MBTI personality information to help you talk through opportunities and worries and your different or similar approaches to money. People with contrasting personality types will approach finances in different ways. It is important to understand your basic personality wiring as it pertains to money as well as how your spouse approaches things related to money based on the family he or she came from. Find a comfort zone that is good for each of you.

Credit Cards: Minimize or Avoid Use: No Carryover Debt

Dave Ramsey strongly advises living on a cash basis.[24] I agree with his concept and encourage all possible steps to avoid and eliminate debt. At the top of the list to avoid is credit card debt. This debt usually comes with a very high interest rate that is hard to eliminate once a mountain of debt starts to build. In our marriage and most we know, credit cards exist. With travel and e-commerce, credit cards offer convenience. The trick is to not let that convenience enable convenience spending. One way to do that is to have the "plastic" bank card but use it as a debit card that draws immediately from your bank account rather than drawing on credit. With the debit card option, you have the financial tool needed for many e-commerce and travel needs, like renting a car, without running up credit debt. A social worker friend who strongly lives by the cash only way pointed out that in a project she was familiar with, one group of people was given $100 cash and encouraged to get the most out of it. Another similar group was given $100 of credit with the requirement that they pay it all back within thirty days. Both of these groups had the appearance of being cash based. However, the cash group got more for their money. There is something about having to pull currency out of a purse or wallet that makes the decisions more disciplined. Also, these days, credit card companies use attractive lures to get people to sign up, especially travel miles. That one-time bonus is a door to a dangerous credit debt trap. Don't fall for these teasers.

Big Item Number 1: Cars

Major purchases like cars and homes are important milestones for a family. We need transportation and shelter. Most couples face the transportation challenge first with the idea of owning a home as a future aspiration. The goal we encourage couples to strive for early in their marriage is to eliminate car debt then enjoy life without car loans for the rest of their lives. There are a couple of steps that can be powerful toward that goal.

---

[24] Dave Ramsey, "15 Practical Budgeting Tips," https://www.daveramsey.com/blog/the-truth-about-budgeting, 2019.

First, if you come into marriage with two cars, one from each of you, find a way to reduce to one car. I know not everyone can do this. But if you live in a place with public transportation, try to do this. Reducing to one car was a big step in our marriage toward freedom from car payments. We carpooled to work in our first year when we lived in a suburb and worked in a city. Later as we began our family, Frances had the car for family needs while I carpooled or used public transportation to work. Later on, I used an old bike to ride to a train station, accepting a ride from Frances in bad weather. If you can, get by with one car.

Second, look at a car for what it really is: a transportation tool that is to serve you. Avoid paying for a prestige car that costs much more than basic transportation. A friend of mine describes his experience toward freedom from car payments. He and his wife looked at what they were paying for transportation and realized that it was far more than they needed to spend. They had two nice vehicles and were still paying on them. They decided to sell both, even though one sold for less than they owed. Swallowing that cost was part of the price of independence from car debt. He says he was worried about what his friends at work would say when he showed up with an older vehicle. He quickly found that nobody cared. He also describes how good it felt to walk into a car dealer with cash in hand to buy what they really needed. Later his friends at work found out that he had no car payments and were envious. Get the car you need and not the one your ego temps you to buy.

Third, after you get free of car payments, save for your next car. In effect, make payments to yourself. After a period of time, you will have the cash in reserve for any needed car replacement, removing a major headache that burdens many people.

Finally, if you are more mature in marriage with children, your kids do not need a car. I watch with amazement how many children at our local school drive to school instead of riding a bus. There is an abundance of nice cars in that student lot. I suspect many families face budgets tight enough that doing without that car expense would be a plus. Our kids learned to drive in the family station wagon. A secondary benefit from that was that their friends were not aching for a joy ride in the old Ford Country Squire. This reduced burden on our children and saved us money. Think hard about incurring the cost and risk of teenage car ownership. Most of the time, they do not need it and will be fine without it.

Putting these factors together, you can save over $600 per month or over $7,000 per year by avoiding a second car and going for a more modest car.[25] This amount plus the $5,000 per year saved by avoiding purchased fancy coffee and lunch at work brings a potential "good stewardship" potential to $12,000 per year. This money is available for some kind of long-term savings. I will add more to this total as we go.

Homeownership: Balancing Common Sense and the American Dream

Homeownership is a commendable dream and goal. The important boundary here is similar to decisions about car ownership. Get what you need, not what your ego says you want. With homes, the challenge even is greater because there are many arguments about the financial advantage of homeownership as an investment. Real estate agents will eagerly give you tools to calculate the maximum home you can afford. Early in our marriage, we listened to those arguments and bought the most home that we could afford. In retrospect, that was the biggest financial mistake of our marriage. We owned prestige homes that were much more expensive than what our family basically needed. At times, that put stress on our budget and unspoken stress in our marriage. It took us ten years to figure out how silly that was. About that time, we moved to a new city and made the conscious decision to buy less home than we could afford. That allowed us to put a greater percentage down and reduced the amount of debt we owned. Less home meant less insurance, less maintenance, and fewer utilities, saving significant money. In 2018, the average home mortgage payment was $1,022 monthly.[26] Cutting 25 percent from that amount can save $3,000 per year on the mortgage alone. Add in other savings

---

[25] Based on average car payment reported by Edmunds of $479 in 2018 plus insurance and license. https://www.thebalance.com/average-monthly-car-payment-4137650
[26] https://www.thebalance.com/average-monthly-mortgage-payment-4154282

that come from owning a more modest home can bring another $1,000 in savings from insurance, taxes, maintenance, and utilities. This $4,000 on housing added to early $12,000 per year from cars and workplace food and beverage purchases brings the savings potential to $16,000 annually. Your IRA will really like that!

The decision to live with less home than you can afford sets the stage for getting to a point without a mortgage payment. For us, we had a fifteen-year plan that began with less home and a conscious strategy to pay down as much debt as we could. Our goal was to pay off the mortgage before our first child entered college. We did not quite make that date but were not far off. Beyond the steps already described, the key action was to use any unexpected money, a bonus or gift, to reduce the debt. I still remember the feeling of walking from the train to my Chicago office the day we wrote the payoff check for our home. Believe me: that feels good! By beginning early in marriage with a realistic approach to homeownership, reaching a point in life with no mortgage is much more possible than advertised.

Long-Term Financial Planning and Goal Setting

Savings is not dismal. It is empowering and makes dreams come true. Begin early forming long-term goals as a couple. This will add purpose and direction to your financial stewardship. After we had been married about fifteen years, I heard a talk by former Notre Dame football coach Lou Holtz on goal setting. He is known for his testimony about looking at his life at a low point at age twenty-eight. He is reported to have come up with 107 ambitious goals.[27] That speech made me think, *I don't have any long-term goals like that.* I had plenty of random wishes and dreams but not the focus of Coach Holtz. I sat down and wrote a list of about twenty-five things representing a wide spectrum of my life. The list included things like maintaining a healthy marriage and being a good father to our five

---

[27] Fred Whelen and Gladys Stone, "Lou Holtz's Compelling Quest to Do 107 Things Before He Died," *Life Magazine,* https://www.huffingtonpost.com/fred-whelan-and-gladys-stone/lou-holtzs-compelling-que_b_794675.html, 2010, Last updated December 7, 2017

kids. It included areas of service like the goal to become a permanent deacon or to lead a local United Way. It included personal things like good health and running a marathon. There were fun things like owning a convertible or taking a Caribbean vacation. Core to the money part was the goal to pay off the mortgage and have adequate savings to be able to retire before age sixty. Ten years later, nearly everything on the list had been accomplished. The list provided focus for us as a couple that included a direction for our spending, saving, and overall financial stewardship. A fruit of that direction was joy. The joy came from less worry because we did have some reserve and continually added to that. The joy came because the goals were not all austerity. There were fun things like the convertible and vacation. There was the special joy of getting to the goals together. Reaching the financial goals was a particular joint win that was only possible together. Doing this kind of goal setting and planning early will help you tremendously and strengthen unity in your marriage.

With financial direction and savings, much is possible. Going back to the potential to add $16,000 per year to an individual retirement account (IRA) from savings I described, you can be a millionaire in less than thirty years. This assumes that each year you add the equivalent of $16,000 in today's dollars to your IRA and only get return equal to inflation of 3 percent. With some effort in investment planning, a much higher return is likely. With a typical investment return, the time to $1 million will be much less than thirty years. You can do this, but you have to start now.

Charity and Its Place in Stewardship

Charity and giving back to God are moral musts. Far back in our faith history, our ancestors had a personal relationship with God that recognized that all that we have are God-given gifts. In Genesis 28:20–22, Jacob, the father of Israel, established the principle of giving back a portion of what we have to God. The tradition of tithing or giving 10 percent of what we earn, gain, or grow to God was core to life in the God/human covenant.

> Jacob then made this vow: "If God will be with me and
> protect me on this journey I am making and give me food

to eat and clothes to wear, and I come back safely to my father's house, the LORD will be my God. This stone that I have set up as a sacred pillar will be the house of God. Of everything you give me, I will return a tenth part to you without fail."

As in much of the Old Testament, Jacob is expressing a relationship of mutual giving. As he petitions God for what he needs, he promises to recognize those gifts by giving a portion back. In the context of our marriages, what greater need could we express than to have a good and holy marriage? When we are given that gift, it is right to give back to God some gift of gratitude for that blessing.

Later that principle of tithing was an integral part of the Law of Moses. Leviticus 27:30–32 says,

All tithes of the land, whether in grain from the fields or in fruit from the trees, belong to the LORD; they are sacred to the LORD. If someone wishes to redeem any of the tithes, the person shall pay one fifth more than their value. The tithes of the herd and the flock, every tenth animal that passes under the herdsman's rod, shall be sacred to the LORD.

The Law continued the definition of tithe as 10 percent and made it clear that we are to give of our best. That means we give our "first fruits" or best, not the leftovers. In marriage, that means that charity has a place at the top of our budget, not at the bottom. We give always and not just when we have something left. Leviticus 23:9–10 says,

The LORD said to Moses: Speak to the Israelites and tell them: When you come into the land which I am giving you, and reap its harvest, you shall bring the first sheaf of your harvest to the priest.

In Deuteronomy 26:12, scripture describes the practical direction and intent of the tithe.

When you have finished setting aside all the tithes of your produce in the third year, the year of the tithes, and have given them to the Levite, the resident alien, the orphan and the widow, that they may eat and be satisfied in your own communities.

The words describe the path of the tithe being multidirectional. Those sharing the tithe include the Levite, or priest, as well as the "alien," orphan, and widow. This is aligned perfectly with the stewardship guidance that many parishes use. They begin with the 10 percent tithe then advise directing it by giving 5 percent to the church and 5 percent to other charities.

Jesus takes the concept of giving back to God out of the realm of legal definition and makes it a matter of heart in Matthew 23:23. His point is that charity is not limited by a definition with an easy stopping point. By that I mean, we cannot mechanically give 10 percent and say we're done.

Woe to you, scribes and Pharisees, you hypocrites. You pay tithes of mint and dill and cummin, and have neglected the weightier things of the law: judgment and mercy and fidelity. [But] these you should have done, without neglecting the others.

In giving back to God in our modern context of charity, we are called to give with compassion to those in need. We are told to respond with full heart in a human way and not simply pay a tax then close our eyes to those in need. This charity without limit that Jesus presents is much harder than a fixed threshold of 10 percent. Coming to terms with the proper amount of charitable giving for your family is a core challenge in marriage. But as we manage our finances, the charitable giving component of our budget can be a powerful marriage builder. Like other important parts of a good marriage, charity takes communication, willingness to give, and understanding.

Many couples use a tithe as a guide. However, the answer for you may be more or less at this point of your life. If your charitable giving has not been much, moving immediately to 10 percent may be more than your budget can stand. If that is the case, start on a path of steady increases over time aimed to reach 10 percent over several years. That is the path Frances and I followed. You will be amazed, as we were, how fast you can reach a tithing level of charity. Working as husband and wife to share with others to make the world better is a source of joy in marriage.

Closing this section on finance and marriage, I repeat that financial unity is a major factor in the comfort of marriage and its ultimate sustainability. Not coming to a unity point can lead to disaster. Getting to a unity point can lead to an abundance of joy.

Chapter 8

<hr />

SEX IS ALL IT IS
CRACKED UP TO BE

It might seem odd that I make the enthusiastic statement about sex to lead off this chapter. The Catholic Church has been a consistent target for jokes about its suppression of sex. Imaginations that the church encourages sex solely as a means to make more Catholics are far from true. Furthermore, the picture that the church is a collection of celibate guys wanting to take the fun out of life for the rest of us is far from true.

Scripture gives a foundation for the beauty of marital love and physical relations. From the closing words of Genesis 2:24–25, we hear,

> That is why a man leaves his father and mother and clings to his wife, and the two of them become one body. The man and his wife were both naked, yet they felt no shame.

We appreciate this gift of human creation as sexual beings. God inspires scripture writers to use the sexual joy of marital relations in fidelity as an image to describe God's love for us. Some of the words would make grocery store romances seem tame. For example, about a woman of desire, Song of Songs 7:7–12 says,

> How beautiful you are, how fair, my love, daughter of delights! Your very form resembles a date-palm, and your

breasts, clusters. I thought, "Let me climb the date-palm!
Let me take hold of its branches! Let your breasts be like
clusters of the vine and the fragrance of your breath like
apples, And your mouth like the best wine—What flows
down smoothly for my lover, gliding over my lips and
teeth. I belong to my lover, his yearning is for me. Come,
my lover! Let us go out to the fields, let us pass the night
among the henna.

About the man of desire, Songs 5:10–16 says,

My lover is radiant and ruddy; outstanding among
thousands. His head is gold, pure gold, his hair like palm
fronds, as black as a raven. His eyes are like doves beside
streams of water, Bathing in milk, sitting by brimming
pools. His cheeks are like beds of spices yielding aromatic
scents; his lips are lilies that drip flowing myrrh. His arms
are rods of gold adorned with gems; His loins, a work of
ivory covered with sapphires. His legs, pillars of alabaster,
resting on golden pedestals. His appearance, like the
Lebanon, imposing as the cedars. His mouth is sweetness
itself; he is delightful in every way. Such is my lover, and
such my friend, Daughters of Jerusalem!

In Proverbs and the New Testament letter of Paul to the Ephesians, the
sensual joy is connected to fidelity. This is a fact that long married couples
can attest to: a lifetime of fidelity enriches sexual pleasure.

Proverbs 5:15–19 says,

Drink water from your own cistern, running water from
your own well. Should your water sources be dispersed
abroad, streams of water in the streets? Let them be yours
alone, not shared with outsiders; Let your fountain be
blessed and have joy of the wife of your youth, your lovely
hind, your graceful doe. Of whose love you will ever have
your fill, and by her ardor always be intoxicated.

St. Paul also connects the essential ingredient of self-giving as a path to sexual joy.

Ephesians 5:28–31 says,

> So [also] husbands should love their wives as their own bodies. He who loves his wife loves himself. For no one hates his own flesh but rather nourishes and cherishes it, even as Christ does the church, because we are members of his body. For this reason a man shall leave [his] father and [his] mother and be joined to his wife, and the two shall become one flesh.

Many of these words of scripture were captured by Pope John Paul II, now recognized as St. John Paul II. His words known as the Theology of the Body are a good place to appreciate the church's regard for the combination of the moral, ethical, ethos side of marital sex with the sensuous eros side. Early in his years as pope, in the late 1970s and early 1980s, he gave 129 talks describing our existence as sexual beings. He talked about the gift and purpose of human existence. He talked about the role of our human bodies in God's plan. He reinforced the church's teaching about love and sexuality in God's plan. His entire message was delivered in a modern context.

Others have taken the content of his talks and formed them into various educational packages, but there is nothing like the original. The talks are available online and free. They are worth the read. What comes out in the pope's actual words is a very human message. The words reveal the pope's life experience as an athlete, a poet, a playwright, a restaurant worker, a philosopher, a traveler, and a youth minister. He expresses the joy of being alive as human men and women fully equipped with sexuality.

From a church teaching standpoint, the pope reminded us that Catholic Theology of the Body rests on important and joy-filled truths. Men and women are created in the image of God. We cannot live without love. The body is a good and important part of our existence. Man and woman from the beginning form a communion of persons that is an expression of God's communion with humanity. St. John Paul II says,

> The human body includes right from the beginning … the capacity of expressing love, that love in which the person becomes a gift—and by means of this gift—fulfills the meaning of his existence.[28]

As he addresses sexual relations, he says that "man and the woman express their willingness to become 'one flesh' and express in this sign the reciprocal gift of masculinity and femininity as the basis of the conjugal union of the persons." In doing so, his background as a playwright and artist comes through when he conveys the joyful experience of sex in marriage. "Marriage is the meeting place of eros with ethos … in the heart of man and of woman, as also in all their mutual relationships." What he is saying is that in marriage, we have the wonderful intersection of the moral and the sensual. Both are good. If we are looking for a bit of the innocence and joy of Eden, I cannot think of a better place to look.

Those who wait until their wedding day to experience sexual intercourse set themselves up for that day to be a day of wonders that those who have been sexually active before marriage will never experience. Chastity before the wedding adds to the anticipation and completeness of the day. Even if you have had sex before, even if you are living with your fiancé now, making the remaining days before your wedding a period of chaste anticipation of your wedding day will add to the joy of the day. I remember the unexpected and great feeling that touched me the night before our wedding. It was a prelude to our first night together. I was consumed with the unity we were about to have blessed by church and society. I was not focused on the impending reality of sex. But that evening, perhaps brought on by teasing from Fran's male cousins, I realized that among the great things that were about to happen was that I would discover sex. The discovery was worth the wait. I hear that same emotion expressed by others who waited for their wedding day.

Since that day, I have come to appreciate the gift of bodies that we made to each other. It is a complete giving that includes unity in every aspect of life.

---

[28] Pope John Paul II, "The Man-Person Becomes a Gift in the Freedom of Love," General Audience in St. Peter's Square, January 16, 1980

But the gift of bodies is special. In making the gift of our bodies to each other in a truly sacramental, covenant way, we do it without reservation. As we come to each other completely exposed and vulnerable, we know no shame and feel no fear because we know that the other will not leave or ever run because of who we are. This is covenant! In that covenant sex is a gift to each other, not something to have or take. Suddenly, many of the worries media express about whether sex will be good or whether we will be good enough are nonexistent.

Into the spiritual realm, I know of no better human experience of complete giving of self than marriage, especially coming to the marriage bed. In the marital act, we can feel connection to the Eucharist when we hear Jesus's words "This is my body which will be given up for you." At a wedding mass, the man and woman making their vows that day are doing the same. It is not in the same way and same magnitude, but nonetheless, it is complete giving. As you gaze on your bride or groom on your wedding day, look at all the beauty, the strength, and the future before you. It is all being given to you. That man or woman will age and change. Life will slowly fade through work, children, joys, and sufferings. But that is all part of the gift of self that we give each other at marriage. Nowhere is it more profound than when the man and woman come together in a sexual union on their wedding day. If it has been years since your wedding day, think back to that day and remember the look of that person before you. Now think back on your years together and remember all that she or he has given to you. Really absorbing the reality of this total gift is humbling.

We get a less sensual but certainly complete look at the moral dimensions of sex in marriage from the Catholic Catechism. One surprising aspect of what the church has to say about sex in marriage is the amount of words devoted to morality and moral limits of sex in marriage in the catechism. The surprising part for a church that is accused of regulating every detail of sex is how little is actually said. The section on sex in marriage is limited to a few pages. It includes teaching on the purpose of marriage and importance as the foundation of the church: the domestic church. It reminds us in the section title "The Love of Husband and Wife" (2,360–2,363) of the necessary elements of marital sex being unity and openness to life. It reminds us of monogamous fidelity. These may seem like basic and obvious points about marriage, but they are differentiating from many other ways that people relate sexually, even in marriage. Think about Jesus's teaching that overturned many aspects of man/woman relations of his day. He reaffirmed the permanence of marriage established at creation when he overturned the Mosaic Law allowing divorce. He eliminated the allowance for a man to have more than one wife. He lived and taught the equality of man and woman in contrast to the practice of wives as property. He provided the foundation for the teachings of St. Paul that describe roles of wife and husband being based on total giving of each to the other loving each other as one loves one's own body. The concise words of the catechism convey this new covenant Christian way of living in marriage.

Part of realizing total joy in marriage is to engage in sex without an ounce of guilt or shame. This is the bit of Eden there for us. This does not come naturally for many since sex is not often a constructive topic discussed by parents with their children. Often in preparing couples for marriage, I have a female social worker join me for discussion of the couples' premarriage inventory. I remember one session with a couple that seemed very savvy to the world. They really were the high school quarterback marrying the cheerleader. When we finished that session, my social worker partner asked, "Is there anything else you would like to discuss?" The bride answered, "It's just the sex thing!" On further questioning, we found that this woman's only sex education from her home was from her mother. The instruction was simply "Don't do it!" As we continued, the social worker gently conveyed the beauty of sex that, among other things, was part of making her own existence happen.

Many of us come into marriage with little sex education or experience. If we get to the wedding day as virgins, we probably had considerable moral guidance that helped us get there. It is understandably hard to shift immediately from "Don't do it" to "naked without shame" in a sensuous union. While this is not intended to be a sex manual, some words are appropriate to convey how few the actual boundaries of sexual experience within marriage are. The opportunities for sexual adventure and excitement for husband and wife within marriage is grand. The test is this: is what you and your spouse are about to do something that will bring unity to you as man and wife, and is this action open to the possibility of new life? Much is possible under this test.

The sexual part of marriage is not something that will be fully mature on the wedding day. As married couples, we learn and grow together. A priest friend occasionally talks to our marriage preparation groups about the parallels between growth as a priest and growth as a married couple. Forming the marriage is only the beginning in the same way that ordination day begins a life of priesthood. We are always a work in progress. This includes living the sexual intimacy part of marriage. Our experiences with each other, imaginations, and ideas from the world around us will expand and shape our sexual experiences. You will learn that in a healthy, married, sexual relationship, your adventure and joy will surpass anything experienced by sexual adventurers outside marriage. Tapping into romantic stories, exciting movies, and sex manuals have a place in marriage within the tolerance of the couple. Look particularly for things that help you build romance as well as physical sex. As you discover ideas, find those that feel right for the two of you that are desired by both aimed to build unity emotionally, spiritually, and physically. By "romance," I mean those things that are special and dear to your mate that take some effort as a real gift of yourself. This does not mean spending money. It can be as simple as a well-planned meal or day together that gives you as a couple special escapes from all the ordinary times of life. These romantic things could stand on their own as a gift without sex. In marriage, we have the added opportunity to include physical sex as part of this romantic gift. In doing this, *always* think of what you can give your spouse rather than focusing on what you want in terms of physical pleasure. Imagine how joy filled a marriage can be when man and woman both put their focus on how they can be a gift to the other. There is no better formula to end up with joy and pleasure for yourself than total giving to your spouse.

Your marriage commitment to each other gives the privilege of drawing from that inventory of exciting and erotic ideas to explore on your own very sweet ground. Others outside the "naked without shame" world of marriage cannot experience this in the same glorious way. Every couple will have a different level of comfort. Also, your comfort level with resources that help you explore possibilities will grow with time together. Not everything within these resources will meet the moral test of unity and openness to life. This is where a couple solid in a covenant marriage and true to God-given morals will be able to extract what is morally right and discard the rest. The key is to grow together. This means talking about sex and expressing what you like and how you feel. As hard as it is for some to talk about sex, husband and wife must do it. As discussed in the section on personality types, this is easier for some than others. However, your sex life is important enough that you need to do this. One big advantage of natural family planning (NFP) that I will address later is that using NFP forces a couple to talk about sex. The basic conversation about where you are in the fertility cycle is a start to a deeper conversation about romance and sex.

We are gifts to each other. A popular television show that I liked at first but came to dislike is *Everybody Loves Raymond*. On the surface, this looked like a good show. It involves a Catholic couple with kids who live with daily connection to their extended family. They remain active in church, and all looks good. Where I began to dislike the show is when I thought about how the father, Raymond, is continuously depicted as an oaf. Furthermore, when I thought about how marital sex is portrayed in the show, it was awful. This show is no model of a man and woman living as gifts for each other. Instead, sex is something that Ray's wife has that Ray wants. However, he is only granted access to it on special occasions or after extended begging. Sooner or later, a man like Ray will give up or—worse—go elsewhere.

Our gift of self to our spouse takes some investment. If we do not spend the effort to continue to nurture this gift to our spouse, our marriage will miss some wonderful joy that can be there. If we are good, healthy people with no physical impediment to offering ourselves sexually to each other, we need to spend the effort to keep the gift alive. It is easy to get lazy and let this aspect slip into a low priority task. I remember some words from a teacher couple that worked with Frances telling us about some of the best parts of marriage. They were obviously talking about bedtime. They said it is the best of times not just because of the obvious physical experience of sex but because of all that closeness does to enhance communication beyond the sex experience. Scientists have found biochemical facts that explain some of this. When we have sex, our brains secrete a chemical called dopamine that boosts energy and focus. This is an internal version of rose-colored glasses. The whole experience brings pleasure and makes us feel good. In humans, a second chemical, called oxytocin, is secreted. Oxytocin causes us to focus on our partner. Oxytocin is a boost to monogamy, making our spouses look increasingly good to us. In Ginny Graves's article "All about Attraction," she describes how orgasm leaves us intoxicated via dopamine and the postsex snuggling turns oxytocin loose, making us even more attached to our spouses.

Our bodies are made to bring us together via sex beyond just the physical act. Given this aspect of our physical makeup, sex is not just a benefit of marriage; it is a strengthener and builder of marriage. The chemistry of our makeup magnifies our unity beyond the immediate feeling of sex.[29] We cannot get lazy and let this part of married life slip away. For us of faith, thank you, God, one more time for leaving us this gift of Eden! Genesis 1:31 says, "God saw all that He had made, and behold, it was very good."

Things That Erode the Glory of Sex in Marriage

For all the wonder and goodness that comes with our sexuality expressed in marriage, the world is full of things that can turn this gift into destructive force. When our first parents brought shame into the world by choosing their own desires above God's way, the course of human history from that point forward has been filled with human actions to choose ways that distort the intent of the things of creation. At the top of the list of good things used in destructive ways is sex. The fire of passionate desire leading to a destructive end is not new to our time. Sirach 23:16 says, "Burning passion is like a blazing fire, not to be quenched till it burns itself out; One unchaste with his kindred never stops until fire breaks forth."

---

[29] Ginny Grarves, "All About Attraction," *The Science of Marriage, Time Magazine Special Edition.* 2017

We know the feeling or emotion under the name of lust. Lust redirects sexual desire from its presence in Original Innocence to a place of shame. As men and women living together as sexual beings, we are changed when we cross the line from love-based desire to lust-based desire. When we cross that line, no longer are man and woman gifts to each other. They become objects of desire for use and pleasure. Instead of the purpose of our sexual unions being unity and openness to life, lust makes the purpose of the sexual union fulfillment of sexual need. The gift or giving part is gone. It is all about getting and taking. When this happens, gone is dignity, gone is openness to creation of life, and gone is real communion of persons.

Before getting into the consequences of lust, there is merit in talking about what lust is not. People sometimes burden themselves with guilt over feelings that are just part of our basic human makeup. First, lust is not admiration of beauty. A person can look at, admire, and even have good feelings upon seeing an attractive man or woman. Admiration of beauty without any desire to possess is not lust. Lust is not merely looking at or admiring the human body. Lust sets in when we take a step across the line into desire and want. St. John Paul II in his Theology of the Body talks addresses nudity in art.[30] He differentiates between admiration of the naked body as a part of inspiring visual art and degradation or use and exploitation. He contrasts nudity in art, some of which he was a party to restoring in the art of the Vatican, to exploitation of nudity in less tasteful forms where initiation of desire is an intent or the model is used without true respect for the human spirit encased in a body.

Lust is not enjoying the company of friends of the opposite sex. Mature couples in deep covenant marriages know that friends of both sexes are healthy. In a good marriage, these friendships are openly discussed and recognized, bringing benefits to all involved. They fully trust themselves and their spouses to have friendship relationships that are in no way romantic. So again, the boundary line leading to lust is the transition from admiration

---

[30] Pope John Paul II, "The Human Body, Subject of Works of Art," April 15, 1981; "Reflections on the Ethos of the Human Body in Works of Art," April 22, 1981; "Art Must Not Violate the Right to Privacy," April 29, 1981; "Ethical Responsibilities in Art," May 6, 1981; General Audience, St. Peter's Square

and appreciation to desire and want. It is desire and want that lead to action plans and movement into adultery. Inside, you will know the difference. Pay attention to your conscience, and joy in marriage will prosper.

When someone moves from love to lust, they are in for disappointment. Lust can never satisfy. Succumbing to lust leads to destruction without satisfaction. There are the obvious tragedies of broken marriages and families. There are also the tragedies of exploitation and abuse. But there are the personal tragedies for the ones who are driven by lust. They become alone and lost. They become unfulfilled. They lose whatever was good in their human relationships because they have spent their energy on something opposed to love and covenant. When energy is spent on things other than love, love loses. Like many things, we are not capable of doing everything our emotions desire. We have to choose. When we choose the lust-driven path, we don't have enough energy left for anything like a covenant commitment. It is impossible to find happiness outside love. Do you know any sexually permissive person who "gets enough" to be forever happy?

For most of us who enter marriage with the true intent to live a life of covenant love, the extremes described in the last few paragraphs are not in our field of view when we marry. If we keep our focus on our commitment of love, we can remain strong in our marriage and continue to experience the joys that come with that. However, I suspect all people have urges and temptations that invite us to approach and occasionally cross the line from love to lust. I know the feeling. There are times when the ordinary world around us is filled with suggestions. These trigger the chemical reactions within us, building an emotion that simply wants sex. That is wired into us. That dopamine that is there to boost desire does exactly that. Unchaste desire creeps into our heads, and the early steps toward adultery in the heart get underway. St. John Paul II takes the courageous step of saying that adultery can even happen within a marriage in the heart toward one's spouse. He is talking about moving from focusing on making ourselves a gift to our spouse and reverting to using that person as a convenient object for pleasure.

Adultery is more than just having an affair. It is other things that can take the place of spouse in our life. I don't need to say that having sex with someone other than your spouse is wrong and destructive. That's obvious. What is less obvious is how other forms of diversion can be destructive to a marriage as well. Most common is pornography or even softer diversions that can be used to satisfy our needs for emotional and sexual satisfaction. The woman who gets her emotional fulfilment from a romance novel instead of working to find fulfilment in her physical relationship with her husband is in the same boat as the man who looks at an adult magazine instead of spending the effort developing a satisfying relationship with his wife. In both cases, the spouse is replaced by another vehicle for satisfaction. The relationship suffers. Romance novels and adult stories that focus on excitement in marriage are not bad in themselves. Like so many things that humanity has created, the judgment is in the use. If these romantic and/or exciting things are in the comfort zone for both and contribute to building unity open to life through sexual adventure within the couple, great and good. But if these things are used by one because working on the relationship with the other is too much work, they are not good. Whether it is romance novels or flirting at the office, actions that are a substitute for making the effort to find satisfaction with our spouse are destructive.

The challenge is to recognize when that line from love to lust is approaching, come to our senses, and take action to keep us in a relationship where actions are driven by giving and love. By remembering the joy we have in our marriage and the richness that comes with unity and openness to life, we can control our passions and redirect them to a constructive course that builds rather than destroys our marriage. A covenant commitment to our spouse and God can keep us on the right side of that line. This sometimes takes work and certainly takes two. If one degrades or abandons full commitment to the covenant, including the sexual part, it is much harder for the other to remain on the right side of the line.

While I cannot condone anyone who has an affair, uses pornography for satisfaction, or in some other way lives a fantasy life in lieu of working on their marriage, I do understand how people get there. Sometimes the feeling of abandonment by spouse and loneliness is so great that things happen. In listening to people talk about how they got into an extramarital affair, I cannot remember anyone saying that it was because the sex with the other person was great. What I do hear are things like "He (or she) listened to me. He (or she) made time for me." I hear words that say, "I felt abandoned." Most people who have told me stories like this are not serial cheaters. They were in such an emotional pit that the other person provided a lifeboat. As loving spouses, we need to always be the lifeboat for our spouses. Remaining connected, including sexually, is a good way to do it.

This all boils down to contrast and choice in the heart between the contrasts of love and lust.

Love	Lust
giving	possessing
mastery of self	out of control
satisfaction	disappointment
divine communion	abandonment
attraction	compulsion
creative	destructive
fertile	poison

By being consciously aware of the reality that lust will be around us now and then, we can steer ourselves clear of disaster. This, like everything else in marriage, takes work and commitment. But like everything else in the realm of Original Innocence, it is very worthwhile to make and live that choice.

Making sex better and better over the years really is possible. I have heard a story told to young men about to be married that goes something like this: "Get a jar and put a penny in it for each time you have sex in your first year of marriage. After that, take a penny out each time you have sex. You will never go broke!" From what I hear from long-lived marriages as well as social scientists, that story is a myth. There is a cycle of romance, disillusionment, and joy in marriage, but there is an abundance of good news regarding romance and sex over the years.

Most couples on their wedding day are probably in that romance stage. But life goes on with the normal pattern of struggles of early life with struggles to find a career, raise kids, and manage tight money. We also get quickly to a point where the newness wears off. I have even heard people describe moments when they wonder, *Why did I ever do this?* As marriage continues, along come children who move from adorable babies to teenagers before we know it. Then there come aging parents and our own diminishing physical bodies. All of these changes bring some form of disillusionment from the romantic vision we had before we got married. It is hard to imagine getting old when we get married. Our parents and grandparents look old beyond any extrapolation of ourselves that we can make. Particularly evident is that those "old" people certainly are past the point of having and enjoying sex. There are plenty of cartoon images of old people attempting to be sexual that provide comic relief for those who see them. But there are plenty of facts to prove that those pictures are wrong!

Beyond the humor, there is plenty of information to prove that human beings can remain sexually active well into senior life. What is evident is that the couples who put the effort into continually growing in their marriage, including letting their sex life evolve and mature as they mature, will live joy-filled senior years in their covenant marriage. This is not intended to be a full essay on senior sex. What I do want to convey is that with changes in life and commitment of man and woman, changes can bring good things to their sex life. The changes in the first few decades of marriage come from responsibilities and challenges of raising a family. Time for romance and sex needs some planning. Even then, the stresses of life can affect the basic biology of sex. Later, kids leave home and direction in life is pretty well set, leaving some times and places for romance that were hard to find with a house full of kids. As years add up, menopause happens, and with it, the efforts of natural family planning become history. With retirement, even more time is available for each other.

Through these stages, a couple can continually choose to give and grow with each other or move apart. The end stories for people are wildly different between people who grow together compared to those who grow apart. Part of growing together is to take full advantage of the communication and understanding of personality that should happen before and early in marriage. Open communication will be the platform to understand physical, emotional, and circumstantial changes that happen as we age. A full connection emotionally and spiritually feeds the joyous connection of physical sexual connection in old age. Without going deeper into this topic, it is important to understand that couples can enjoy a glorious sex life into old age. Getting to that point means starting at the beginning to have that covenant connection and practical skills of understanding and communication to keep your sex life alive and evolving as you age.

From my perspective and others I know, sex can get better and better over the years. It will change. Frequency and duration will change, but the quality gets better. At thirty and forty years married, there is a deep appreciation of the person who has been there with you through the years. This appreciation feeds a new batch of those body chemicals that give us those rose-colored glasses that make husband or wife more attractive to each other than ever before. The joyous, physical part of marriage for those ever giving to each other in covenant just keeps getting better and better!

Chapter 9

PARENTING: KEEPING MARRIAGE AS PRIORITY 1

Openness to be a partner with God in bringing new life is a fundamental part of marriage. In the Western world, openness to children is becoming an increasingly neglected part of society. The magazine *Forbes* in 2012 reported that much of the Western world is not reproducing at a rate to sustain its population. The replacement rate or total fertility rate (TFR)— the reproduction rate that keeps a population stable—for developed countries is 2.1. In the US, the total fertility rate is 2.0, with that level sustained largely by Hispanic immigrants who lead the country in birth rates.[31] In Western Europe, the figures are more severe. For example, Germany has a TFR of 1.4, Holland has 1.8, Belgium has 1.8, and Italy has 1.4. With social changes dramatically advancing the state of women in developed countries, women are no longer socially or economically dependent on men. The magazine reports that many women are deciding to either put off getting married or remain single. In Asia, 44.2 percent of Singaporean men and 31.0 percent of women between the ages of thirty and thirty-four remain single. With so much conversation about sustainability when it comes to the environment, the thing we need most for a sustainable society—new human beings—is at risk.

---

[31] Lee Kuan Yew, "Warning Bell for Developed Countries: Declining Birth Rates," *Forbes Magazine,* https://www.forbes.com/sites/currentevents/2012/10/16/warning-bell-for-developed-countries-declining-birth-rates/#5f04fa363641, October 16, 2012

Children are a blessing and source of joy. Listen to what you hear people talk about at work, at church, or just around the neighborhood. You will hear plenty about kids from the mouths of proud parents. Raising a child is the most significant thing we can do as a woman and man united in marriage. We can accomplish things in our work or community. We can build and run a pretty home. But raising children is the part that will establish our lasting legacy, our old-age joy, and contribution to the human race. It will be the thing that we can be proudest of and be the source of joy and satisfaction in our old age beyond any career or other focus.

One of the top reservations that I hear from couples in marriage preparation about having children is how expensive it is to have and raise a child. There is a feeling of "I am not sure we can afford a family." From what I get from popular media, I understand the worry. I have read numerous articles about how expensive it is to have and raise a child. *Money* magazine reported that in 2017, the cost of raising a child was $233,610.[32] They say, "Families with lower incomes are expected to spend $174,690, while families with higher incomes will likely spend $372,210." That's enough to scare off prospective parents. Yet some of the most joy-filled families that I see are not rich. A strong family where love and each person in the family being the primary treasures of living can be very happy. A family that keeps its priorities focused on what is really needed and works together in all aspects of living—food, getting around, child care, housing, sharing bedrooms and education, etc.—can get by on much less than these public figures. In our own family, we saw the real economy of scale that comes with a larger family. Within our family of five kids, we benefited from shared rides, efficient meal preparation, shared bedrooms, and much more. As they grew, we found that the best child care we could get was from our own kids who were better than any babysitter we could hire. Money is not a reason to avoid having children. I cannot remember encountering any parent who wishes that they did not have children. Do not miss this chance!

---

[32] Mahita Gajanan, "The Cost of Raising a Child Jumps to $233,610," *Money Magazine,* http://time.com/money/4629700/child-raising-cost-department-of-agriculture-report/, January 9, 2017

There is no question that being a parent has an impact on a marriage. Much of the public conversation focuses on the immediate impact on marriage as a child arrives. Considered are things like impact on careers, romance, and opportunities for experiences. Researchers have studied how having children affects a marriage. Comparing couples with and without children, researchers found that the rate of the decline in relationship satisfaction is nearly twice as steep for couples who have children as for childless couples. That is depressing and another message to scare prospective parents. No surprise, as we discussed already, with or without children there is a cycle of romance, disillusionment, and joy. It is likely that children arrive sometime after the romance stage, or at least the peak of romance, has ended. The felt satisfaction in marriage declines during the first years of marriage, and if the decline is particularly steep and a covenant commitment is not there, divorce may follow.[33] What is not always reported is that even though measured marital satisfaction of new parents declines, the likelihood of divorce also declines.

Several studies have looked at the long-term path of happiness in marriage. One I find most insightful is a 1987 publication by Michael Argyle called the *Psychology of Happiness*.[34] He looked at several other studies that measured marital happiness over the duration of a marriage. He presented results from four studies that all showed the same pattern. As we come together in marriage, we are happy. But from that day through our first decade of marriage, that happiness slides. Hello, disillusionment. So long, romance. The happiness curve drops sharply into the childbearing years. It takes a brief uptick as the school years begin then bottoms out when our charming kids are teenagers. I don't think it takes deep academic research to figure that trend out. The good news is that from that teenage point forward, the happiness curve climbs to reach heights only experienced in the prechild phase of marriage. A simple response would be "Forget having children. Thank you very much. I'll stick with happiness." But coming back to Matthew Johnson's work that focuses on the evaporation

---

[33] Matthew D. Johnson, Professor of Psychology and Director of the Marriage and Family Studies Laboratory, Binghamton University, State University of New York, *"The Cost of Raising a Child Jumps to $233,610,"* Fortune Magazine, May 9, 2016.
[34] Michael Argyle, *"The Psychology of Happiness,"* Routledge, 1987

of happiness in marriage with children, he recognizes that those who have children do not regret it. He says, "Most mothers (and fathers) rate parenting as their greatest joy."

There are practical changes in life that come with parenting. Worries about the new baby, money challenges, career impacts, and lost sleep are among the obvious. Also there are changes in how we identify ourselves and are identified. Fundamental identities shift from career power woman and beautiful wife to mother and from men's league basketball and beer buddy to stay-at-home dad. On an intimate level, we move from lovers to parents. Matthew Johnson's work on marriage satisfaction for new parents highlights how it is the broad collection of little stuff that can add up to a big slide down the marriage satisfaction ladder. He says, "New parents tend to stop saying and doing the little things that please their spouses. Flirty texts are replaced with messages that read like a grocery receipt." This is where a little caring and work can make your marriage defy this dismal picture. There is no reason flirty texts can't continue. There is no reason you can't make time for your spouse and, when physically ready, for hot, romantic sexual intimacy. The difference is that with young children on board, it takes some conscious planning and effort.

Welcome to the cycle of marriage! Whether it is children or old age, keeping a marriage joyful and growing only comes with commitment.

This book is about joy in marriage and is not a parenting manual. The focus here is to share things that you can do to make your marriage more joy filled in your parenting years. Look to other resources for deeper guidance in the art of parenting. But focusing here just on the health of the marriage, there are some things that I have seen that make a big difference in marital happiness among couples. Keeping a marriage joy filled in the years when couples are meeting the challenges of young children, trying to advance careers, and beginning to feel obligations from aging parents takes work. But it is worth the effort. It is important to start early—even before your wedding. Talk about what you anticipate parenting will be like. Draw especially from your experience growing up. Talk about what will change when you have children and what you will strive to keep the same.

This kind of preparation can provide a very valuable foundation when you have children. You will be able to draw on things you've discussed before the excitement and challenges of the infant at home make your pace so hectic that time for thinking is not always there. Many of the things you do in that first year of parenting will set the pattern for the rest of your years as parents.

The most fundamental pillar of marital happiness is to always put your spouse first. This is a point I discuss with most couples preparing to marry. I want them to think about it now before they have a child in their arms. I see plenty of sad situations where one spouse, usually the mom, turns so much attention to their child that their spouse seems to disappear from the field of concern. To the spouse who has been demoted to second place, this is not a happy place. For a time, that spouse will understand and accept this place, but that won't last. We see the result in society. Many television shows like to present the picture of the single parent with a glowing parent/child bond that is much more entertaining than a story about two middle-aged people raising a family.

Putting your spouse first means making time for romance. Early in our marriage, the couple next door gave us advice that made a world of difference in our marriage. We were living in a suburban neighborhood of mostly young families near the 1970s boomtown Denver. Few people had local family support or much discretionary money. Our neighbors told us to make a weekly, stay-at-home date night. Put the kids to bed, or as they grow older, set them up with their own supper and evening entertainment. Then take a luxury bath and dress up for each other. Prepare a nice meal to enjoy at leisure, separated from the kids. Listen to music, or just talk. Don't take the easy way out and watch TV or a movie. Connect with each other. We started that practice each Saturday night before our first child was born and continue it today in our empty nest years. We make Saturday night sacred. Our kids knew that we would not be running around picking them up from this or that beyond what was absolutely necessary. Our kids learned to respect that since it was the only type of Saturday night they knew until experiencing other families as teens. When our daughters' friends came to pick them up or stay over on a Saturday night, they saw what we did. We had the flattering romantic experience of discovering that one of those teens told our daughter after seeing our Saturday night dinners, "Your parents are so cute."

We see this carrying over into the lives of our children as adults. They don't copy this to the extreme but do respect time for their spouses. We were thrilled when one of our daughters decided with her friends to do something like this on their high school prom evening. Instead of going out to an expensive adult restaurant with all the risks that go with that, they used our home to enjoy a meal they prepared themselves. They were dressed in their prom formals and had a fantastic evening in our sunroom. They got the idea from what they saw in us. You can do this. It will cost you nothing more than your normal cost of living and payoff for a lifetime or more.

Part of putting spouse first comes to a test as children grow. Early on, it is mainly attention. An infant does need a lot of attention. But infants are also learning creatures who will discover how to get attention from a parent. A two-year-old can be very accomplished at parent capture and control. Left to take a purely natural course of undisciplined comfort for the child, the child's control over parents can become damaging to the child and marriage. For example, I run into parents who have children sleeping in the marital bed as a routine for years. I see children who by age four or five are so good at throwing public tantrums that their parents seem powerless in their presence.

This sets up the delicate challenge of responding to real needs of the child without becoming captured by every whimper or want from the child. I do not mean to diminish the need for loving care and attention to the child. What I mean is attend to the real needs. But at other times, let the child do without a comfort that is pure selfish want and not needed. This takes work, and it has to happen as a couple—and happen early. I do not have the exact words to describe how to manage this balance between real need and pure want of discretionary comfort in every household. This is where connection to a church community, family, and friends can help since all parents deal or have dealt with similar challenges. Learn from those who have been there before. Get the support of families like yours who are experiencing the same challenges.

It takes thought and strength as a couple to find a balance. Just having the conversation about how to deal with these challenges with your spouse will help you. Without unity as a couple, guilt or simple fatigue that comes with responsibility can drive one spouse to overly select the child over spouse. Regardless of the exact course you choose as parents to deal with these challenges, it is critical to find a balance that makes your spouse the priority. This includes dedicated time for your spouse. When there is not time, at least let him or her know that you intend to make time.

Keeping the balance where child matters but spouse matters more is an important thing to work on early. The challenges don't stop after the terrible twos. Children can be very good manipulators of parents, working one parent against the other. As parents, husband and wife need to remain closely connected with each other by using every communication and personality preference tool to stay ahead of attempts by a child to work one against the other. Be careful to only commit to major choices regarding something your child wants to do after consultation with your spouse. Let your child see and know that you are going to engage your spouse in an answer before it comes to them. As children grow, the decisions get tougher and more important. When I help parents and godparents prepare for a baptism, I speak to the godparents about an important role they have. I remind them that their job is more than just sending a card at birthdays and Christmas. Their job really matters when that child is twelve and brings home some ideas about things to do and how to live that do not fit the parents' moral values. A twelve-year-old can bring some convincing arguments with emotion that are hard to refute. Parents need to stay the course even though it is not easy when presented with "Everybody else gets to do it." Parents need to be connected but also draw on help of those who can support their effort to raise a morally healthy young adult. Again, this comes back to my discussion about the need for a place for God and the church community in marriage. The couples who draw heavily on this support during their parenting years will find tremendous joy when they get to the day when their dependent children suddenly become their friends. The endpoint of the full-life marriage-happiness curve, which reaches a peak equal to newlyweds, results partly from the joy of experiencing adult children as friends.

Strive to enjoy and love your children. Do not be compelled to be "superparents" with "superchildren." Many parents run around taking children to activity after activity with no time for family. It is easy for children to become oversubscribed with activities. The activities are all good: scouts, sports, arts, and more. The problem is that parents and children become tired and stressed. Most of all, they miss time with each other, especially if there is more than one child. Another source of pressure is the attention given to trying to form a child who will be the top of the world in some way or sometimes multiple ways. It may be to give every push and resource to make the child a star athlete. It may be the same effort to make him or her a top musician or scholar. The family sacrifices time and treasure to give the child every advantage to be the best of the best. Every free moment is spent practicing, traveling, or participating in events or performances. It is possible that your child may be that Olympic champion or top of the Harvard class. But for most people, that will not happen. The sadness comes from all that is missed by this type of intense focus. Families miss time to have fun with each other. Even more, the children miss the chance to be children when they are thrust into an adult competitive world early.

In our family, we limited each child to one activity. That still meant plenty of running around with five children, but we did find time for each other. As adults, we do not hear any regret from our kids that we imposed this limit. They are not Olympic athletes or concert musicians, but they are all good people, and our family remains close and strong. Finding the point of balance between things that you permit your children to engage in and time for family and rest takes every skill a couple has. It needs effective communication that reaches into the heart. The endpoint is to find a point of satisfaction that is unique to you as a couple. When you find it, love will prevail and will last for you as a couple and your children as they become adults. In that place, joy resides!

In the end, raising children is a place where we get to be God's partner in continuing humanity. As we age and mature, we marvel at how fast time goes by. One day, we are on our honeymoon. The next, we are holding an amazing baby. Then we live through the challenges and joys of teen years to discover one day that they are gone. Empty nest is something that many couples both anticipate and dread. Many freedoms and new joys come with having adult children who have adopted our values and are living good lives of their own. As a couple, this can bring experiences that are honeymoon-like that stand behind the Michael Argyle findings that in the postchild years, joy in marriage can approach the joy of early marriage. Many grandparents talk about how they enjoy their grandchildren more than they remember enjoying their own children. Grandparents joke that being grandparents is so much fun because grandparents can experience the joys of a child but hand him or her back to the parents to do the work. Joking aside, part of this is remembering honestly the whole gamut of child raising, including the good times as well as the times when things could have been better. As grandparents, we know there is no do-over but recognize that some of the things learned can benefit the next generation. We carry those hopes to our children as they become parents. Men and women who have lived a covenant marriage open to new life get to enjoy this phase. There will be the feeling similar to what we hope to experience when we meet our Lord at the end of our lives. Matthew 25:23 says, "Well done, my good and faithful servant."

There is joy to living God's plan. God blessed them, saying in Genesis 1:28, "God blessed them and God said to them: Be fertile and multiply; fill the earth and subdue it."

Children bring great joy to marriage. Don't miss it!

Chapter 10

Choosing Natural Family Planning: More than Just Because the Church Says So

God blessed them, saying in Genesis 1:28, "Be fertile and multiply; fill the earth and subdue it. Have dominion over the fish of the sea, the birds of the air, and all the living things that move on the earth." This command completes the God-given twofold theology of living marriage. We are to live marriage in a way that unites us as man and woman as well as being the human vessels in partnership with God in bringing new life to the world.

In preparing couples for marriage, I am usually working in a Catholic environment. Couples come to my classes because they are planning to marry in the Catholic Church. As I mentioned earlier, many of the people in my sessions are not Catholic. They come from many faiths and even non-faiths. When we get to the natural family planning topic, I can feel the wave of "Well, here it comes" combined with a feeling of "We'll hear it, say yes, and be done with it." I get the point. But there is so much more to say in favor of choosing NFP than just the church says so!

General thinking seems to be that artificial contraception in the many available forms is normal and right. In the realm of this general thinking, the couples in my groups probably expect that I am going to promote NFP as the only acceptable way to regulate births, and they are right.

What they become surprised by is that I go far beyond "Do this because the church says so" in making the case for NFP. I make my case based on health advantages, relationship building, and even romance. These arguments carry more weight with most than a pure preaching approach. The result is that people buy in to what I have to say and end up wanting to know more about NFP. Most, I believe, go away with a serious interest in NFP as a way of life in their marriage. By the time you get to the end of this chapter, I hope you will be convinced that NFP is a way to build joy in your marriage. There are many reasons to choose NFP, but among the greatest is that using NFP is a proven significant factor in making a marriage unbreakable.

A modern foundation for a conversation about NFP easily begins with the moral message from Pope Paul VI fifty years ago. He delivered his monumental teaching in a document called *Humanae Vitae*. That communication came at a time when the science of artificial contraception had advanced to a stage where birth control via means like the "pill" were taken for granted. Pope Paul's work aimed to bring morality back into the conversation. His teaching has been praised and criticized ever since. It is most known as the event that cemented the Church's stand against the use of artificial contraception—birth control. In that teaching, Pope Paul brought us back to the basic theology of marriage. He described the marital sex act reminding us of its existence as a gift and of its purpose in God's plan. He said,

> We were given the "twofold significance of the marriage act" and also the "inseparable connection between the unitive significance and the procreative significance of the marriage act."[35]

The Church continues to build on Pope Paul's teaching to this day in a way that is getting more appealing to those beyond the Catholic faith. Following on *Humanae Vitae,* the Church teaches "that in marriage there must be no impairment of its natural capacity to procreate human life."[36]

---

[35] Pope Paul VI, *Humanae Vitae*, Nos. 11 and 12
[36] *Humanae Vitae 11*

This particular doctrine, often expounded by the magisterium of the Church, is based on the inseparable connection, established by God, which man on his own initiative may not break, between the unitive significance and the procreative significance which are both inherent to the marriage act.[37]

This makes sense far beyond Catholic teaching.

God designed marriage as an "intimate partnership of life and love."[38] In God's design, marriage is a unique union of one man with one woman "for the whole of life."[39] Marriage is oriented to the good of the spouses and to the creation and nurture of new human life.[40] Making decisions, therefore, about when and how many children to have in marriage is a sacred responsibility that God has entrusted to husband and wife. This is the foundation of what the Church calls "responsible parenthood," which is the call to discern God's will for your marriage while respecting his design for life and love.

Many people who discount the Church's stand against artificial contraception mistakenly accuse the Church of ignoring the realities of life. The stand against artificial contraception is categorized as against "birth control." That is a false accusation. In its encouragement of responsible parenthood, the church is challenging us to place sexual intercourse in its proper place. First, the proper place is within marriage. Second, it is to be something husband and wife share as a gift to each other. Third, it is integrated with our responsibility to be open to children and be responsible stewards of the lives of children given to us. Part of that loving, giving stewardship of life is using the gift of sexuality in a responsible way. This means family planning within the context of always being open to new life while responsibly planning our families within the

---

[37] *Humane Vitae 12*

[38] Pope Paul VI, "Pastoral Constitution on the Church in the Modern World, Gaudium et spes Promulgated by His Holiness, Pope Paul VI," December 7, 1965, No. 48

[39] Canon Law of the Catholic Church, No. 1055, *The Code of Canon Law*

[40] see Gaudium et spes, no. 48

framework of our natural biology. In our modern world, we have been given abundant knowledge of human biology and reproduction. This has allowed development of many artificial means of birth control as well as knowledge of just as effective natural means of birth control. We are able to understand when pregnancy is most likely to result from the sex act and when it is almost certainly not going to happen. Natural family planning is the way we can experience marital sex that builds our marriage as well as allows us to grow a family in a planned way. It is also fully true to God's plan embedded in our makeup.

Once again, this case for NFP goes beyond any decree of a church and into being a primary means to live a better, healthier life and more joy-filled marriage.

The United States Council of Catholic Bishops says,

> The Catholic Church supports the methods of Natural Family Planning (NFP) because they respect God's design for married love. In fact, NFP represents the only authentic approach to family planning available to husbands and wives because these methods can be used to both attempt or avoid pregnancy.[41]

When learning about NFP, it is important to know the following:

- "Natural Family Planning (NFP) is the general title for the scientific, natural, and moral methods of family planning that can help married couples either achieve or postpone pregnancies."[42]
- "NFP reflects the dignity of the human person within the context of marriage and family life, and promotes openness to life and the gift

---

[41] United States Conference of Catholic Bishops, "Natural Family Planning," http://www.usccb.org/issues-and-action/marriage-and-family/natural-family-planning/, 2019

[42] United States Conference of Catholic Bishops, "What is Natural Family Planning," http://www.usccb.org/issues-and-action/marriage-and-family/natural-family-planning/what-is-nfp/index.cfm, 2019

of the child. By complementing the love-giving and life-giving nature of marriage, NFP can enrich the bond between husband and wife."[43]

- "It is however morally lawful to have 'recourse to the infertile periods' if there are reasonable grounds for spacing births, arising from the physical or psychological conditions of husband or wife, or from external circumstances."[44]

What this says is the Church definitely teaches and supports family planning. It respects the reality of current society that generally favors spacing births and regulating family size. However, this spacing and regulation of family size is to be done naturally within marriage without artificial intervention. Couples today, through a little study and good communication, are able to very effectively plan for growth of their family. For a couple committed to living as a gift to each other with God as a partner, this is a very liberating message!

Yes, natural family planning is the only morally acceptable means of birth control. But there is much more incentive to use NFP. When thinking about sex in marriage and the beauty of that natural act as a mutual gift, I can think of no better way to enrich a love-based marriage than NFP. It is the only unselfish and unity-building means of birth control. Artificial methods are selfish, pleasure based, and often unhealthy for the woman.

The contrast between sex using NFP and sex using artificial contraception is stark.

Sex with Contraception	Sex with Natural Planning
closed to life	open to life
urge based	love based
low value	special gift
slave to impulse	mastery of self

---

[43] United States Conference of Catholic Bishops, "Standards for Diocesan Natural Family Planning Ministry,"
Washington, D.C., 2000
[44] *Humanae Vitae 16*

uses spouse	respects spouse
man's plan	God's plan

The science and art of NFP have come a long way since Frances and I were married. The main coaching Frances got from her mother was "Wait a little before having children." As a husband-to-be, I got no coaching from family, doctor, or church. Our training in NFP came from a pink book on the rhythm method that Frances got from her mother. Fortunately, we were committed to using NFP. We talked about where we were in Frances's fertility cycle and used that as a guide for planning our family. We used a form of the Sympto-thermal method that has advanced considerably since that time. It was effective for us and is reported to be 99 percent effective today.[45] We wanted to wait three years before having a child, and using this method allowed that to happen. When we wanted to begin a family, Frances's body was ready and free from any residual effects of using contraceptives. We conceived right away.

There are several NFP method options. Below are brief descriptions of several. There are abundant printed and internet publications to pursue for more information.[46]

Billings Ovulation Method

Women observe the external mucus that is produced when estrogen is alerting them to approaching ovulation. When progesterone is high, cervical crypts produce a thick mucus that is very difficult for sperm to penetrate and usually not visible externally.

Creighton Model

Women observe the external mucus that is produced when estrogen alerts them to approaching ovulation. When progesterone is high, cervical crypts produce a thick

---

[45] Couple to Couple League, "What is Natural Family Planning," 2019
[46] Catholic Diocese of St. Louis, Source of methods and description, List as of 2018

mucus that is very difficult for sperm to penetrate and usually is not visible externally. The standardization of this model has expanded its use to assist in the diagnosis and treatment of many gynecologic conditions.

Marquette Model

The Marquette Model (MM) system of NFP brings 21st century technology to NFP by using the ClearBlue Easy Fertility Monitor, a device used at home which measures hormone levels in urine to estimate the beginning and end of the time of fertility in a women's menstrual cycle. The information from the monitor can be used in conjunction with observations of cervical mucus, basal body temperature, or other biological indicators of fertility.

Sympto-Thermal Method (Couple to Couple)

Couples are taught to observe mucus and cervix signs, which signal the approach of ovulation, and the temperature sign and other signs, which typically accompany ovulation.

Beyond the moral direction to use NFP, there are three profound advantages to choosing NFP. Most of our marriage prep sessions include quite a few non-Catholics. Most of those fully expect to use artificial contraceptives. For them, simply saying, "Use NFP because the Church says so," is not enough. Over the course of our sessions, I see many of those opinions reversed toward serious consideration of NFP.

Beyond the moral statement pointing toward NFP, the couples that help me with these sessions strongly convey the marriage-building and physical advantages of NFP. First, there is communication and marriage building. NFP provides a vehicle for even the most introverted couples to talk about sex in a way that would not happen otherwise. This makes sex more than just something that happens but brings it to a place of planning and anticipation. The knowledge and anticipation leading to renewal of sexual relations provide a bit of a new honeymoon each month. Second, there are health risks associated with any of the artificial methods. As devices or chemicals are inserted into the woman's body, there are well-documented impacts to health. There is more information available from the couples and organizations that coach NFP as well as generally available sources on the internet or from your doctor to describe the health risks of various artificial contraceptive methods. Third, NFP advances the ability to conceive when a child is wanted. Couples who are trying to conceive will greatly benefit from the knowledge of fertility cycles that come from NFP. NFP is as powerful for those wanting to conceive as it is for those who are not. It worked for us; it can work for you.

In our marriage preparation sessions, couples who hear peers witness to the effectiveness and significant advantages of using NFP end up committed or at least much more open to NFP than they expected coming in. The conversations after NFP presentations are completely focused on desire to learn how to live NFP and do it. The marriage-building and health advantages are so significant that they exceed moral mandates in convincing our couples to consider NFP. We often hear young women say, "Why didn't they tell us this in school?" Whether Catholic or not, couples see the wisdom of using NFP. My objective here is for you to have that same openness and tap into resources that expand on the how-to of using NFP with more detail confirming the effectiveness and health benefits.

Using NFP builds on all that has been discussed in this book about living an unbreakable, joyful marriage. Effective use of NFP requires a true covenant commitment of man and woman. It is true to full inclusion of God as a partner rather than replacing him. NFP requires communication and understanding of each other that is essential in marriage that artificial methods do not nurture. NFP integrates connection to community through networking with other couples who coach use of NFP. NFP brings out the joy of living a sexual relationship in marriage in a giving, nonselfish way. Add all these things up, and you get a marriage that is as close to unbreakable as you can get.

As I said at the start, couples who use NFP have a 97 percent likelihood of being married for life. That's a pretty good reason to bring NFP into your marriage.

Chapter 11

STUFF HAPPENS: RIDING OUT THE HARD SPOTS AND FORGIVENESS

In the chapter that discusses covenant advantage, I presented a list of ugly things that can happen in a marriage. Listed were things that can bring shock and lasting change to a marriage. At the front end of marriage, it is impossible to know what life has in store. But most marriages will experience something from that list. Frances and I have, and most couples we know have too. We have seen firsthand how these tidal waves cause stress and require sacrifice within the boundaries of a marriage. We have also seen that all can be overcome and over time become a source of pride and joy. How a couple overcomes life's big challenges underpins some of the greatest stories told by long-married couples.

The major disruptions or challenges in marriage come in very different ways. Some of the things, such as loss of a child or infertility, come without any action on our part. In effect, we are victims of nature. In such cases, a couple can have a "Why me?" feeling but have support from friends and family. Other things come from events in life that force us to choose a path and adapt. This can be more difficult since there is an element of choice and responsibility. For Frances and me, job-induced moves, including two six-month periods of employment-driven separation, were not anticipated when we got married. Couples with one or both in the military can face challenging and frightening times apart like that. Education-driven separations are not uncommon these days. Some of these conditions can be anticipated before marriage, but the course that a career or military obligation can demand is beyond what we can precisely predict. In most cases, there will be some kind of support, but the couple will still need to draw on their commitment to each other to stay strong during long and lonely periods apart. More challenging are those things that can be attributed to one spouse. Some things like addiction, an affair, or financial ruin often result from the action of one spouse. This type of disruption is the most difficult. There usually is identifiable responsibility that presents the opportunity for one spouse to be seen as guilty and the other as the innocent victim. In these cases, friends and family often encourage the innocent party to cut and run. The couple that decides to stay together in covenant and make changes may not get a lot of support from those around them.

No one wishes for any of these devastating things to happen, but they do. In most cases that I experienced through couples I have listened to, the couple did not see the shock coming. Of those who experienced crushing hardships, some remained married; some didn't. The difference comes from the existence or nonexistence of a true covenant of lifelong fidelity by both parties. It does not work if only one person has it. It takes two. The commitment includes willingness to stay in the marriage and work toward healing. It takes willingness to make repairs to self and willingness to support the other. At times, the couple that perseveres will be swimming upstream against popular opinion in a world that offers easy exits.

Society gives us plenty of ways out of an uncomfortable marriage. I remain a marriage optimist and believe that chances of a couple staying married for life get better all the time. However, the cycle of romance, disillusionment, and joy is real. This cycle, with certain evolution from romance to disillusionment, sets the stage for divorce to happen if the couple is not united in commitment to remain married. Studies suggest that about 10 percent of marriages will fail in the first two years.[47] The pattern of divorce early in marriage is an indication that there is a lack of

---

[47] Lauren Vinopal, "A Year-by-Year Guide to Your Risk of Divorce," *Fatherly Magazine*, https://www.fatherly.com/health-science/twenty-year-guide-divorce-risk/, November 14, 2017

true covenant commitment in some marriages even though all couples say the covenant words at their wedding. With covenant commitment absent, it does not take long for thoughts of splitting to gain ground when hard times happen. Without a covenant commitment, when hardships come, leaving can look better than staying to do the work of healing and growing.

As time in marriage increases, the chances of divorce go down. Beyond the first few years, commitment to stay married increases, partly driven by the presence of children. Census data shows that the average couple begins having children around year 3. As I said in the parenting chapter, children increase relationship stability and decrease divorce risk.

Then comes the infamous seven-year itch. As the happiness in the relationship declines, it approaches the common low point in a marriage. Census data show that this low point in marriage happiness is coincidentally in step with the occurrence of divorce. The average length of a marriage that ends in divorce was 7.2 years in 1990. Now it is a little longer than that.

After the "itch," risk of divorce goes down again. Comparing divorce statistics with the happiness curve shows how couples that have made it to around year 10 generally have come through the abyss and are working in a marriage that is getting progressively more satisfying. Couples that make it to their tenth anniversary experience a lower divorce risk each subsequent year. From then on, the risk is modest, although the recent trend of increased divorce by people in their fifties is troubling. This new trend, "gray divorce," is described by Susan Brown of Bowling Green State University and refers to the divorce rate of adults over fifty doubling between 1990 and 2010. Recent findings from the *General Social Survey* suggest that this period also has a component of extramarital adventure for both genders.[48]

Unhappiness in marriage or the occurrence of one of the tough things can be very lonely for a couple and the man and woman in it. It is not socially

---

[48] Nicholas H. Wolfinger, "America's Generation Gap in Extramarital Sex," Institute for Family Studies, July 5, 2017

acceptable to talk about our marriage difficulties in any forum. It is tough to table these things even in places like the church or family that should be our main lifeboats. There are good programs like Christ Renews His Parish and Marriage Encounter that provide some potential, but it takes courage to engage in those sessions.

Also, I need to say that while I am a vigorous defender of marriage, there are times when divorce is the right answer. If one spouse is repeatedly unfaithful or abusive or living a life of substance abuse with no serious move to rehabilitate, that spouse is showing that he or she is not committed to the marriage. In such a case, the other spouse has little recourse but to seek civil divorce. Also, it is important to know that a divorced man or woman is very welcome in the Catholic Church and its sacraments. A divorced person who has not remarried or entered a sexual union with another is still living with fidelity to that first marriage, even though it has been dissolved in a civil sense.

Also, divorce in itself is not immoral. The moral problem happens when a divorced person remarries and enters a sexual union with another when in the eyes of the church a prior marriage exists. I say "in the eyes of the Church" because the Church assumes that marriage exists whenever a couple presents itself as having been married. When a divorced person comes to the Church wanting a new marriage, the starting point is to respect a former marriage until examination of evidence shows that a real marriage never happened. In cases after a divorce where there is reason to believe that the marriage was formed on false promises, the church offers the compassionate and healing path known as annulment. That annulment petition process provides a thorough examination of the marriage that can find that one party or both did not make a covenant, or sacramental commitment, to the marriage. What the decision rests on is the fact that in many ways what one or possibly both promised on their wedding day turned out to be a lie as evidenced by their life. Perhaps they were not mature enough to marry or were under pressure somehow to marry. In such cases, the Church may issue a decree of annulment that in effect says the persons in the marriage were never married in a sacramental sense and are free to form a real marriage for the first time.

So with divorce readily available and hard times certain, how do couples make it through? The most obvious factor is commitment right from the start to not quit when the going gets tough. When both parties in a marriage have this, the marriage is unbreakable. I have never seen a couple without enough love and strength to recover if they intend to try to recover. Associated with this commitment is the follow-through in the form of work to make wrong things right. This can include counselling or recovery programs. It can include separations for a period of time to make repairs. But a big part of it is the willingness to stay. With that Christlike commitment to stay, a Christlike ability to forgive also must be there.

In her article in *Psychology Today,* Andrea Brandt, PhD and MFT, describes the start of forgiveness as an active choice. She describes how when we are wronged and the initial shock and emotion has subsided, we have a choice to make. Do we forgive the person who hurt us or not? This is not easy, and it is harder for some than others. Think of the personality preference differences of extravert versus introvert or feeler versus thinker. Dr. Brandt also reminds us what forgiveness is not. It does not justify or excuse the other person's actions. It does not mean that the wronged person can or should forget what happened. She also makes the important point that forgiveness is not something we do for the other person. We do it for ourselves. By forgiving, we accept the reality of what happened and find a way to live in a state of resolution with it.

Real forgiveness for something that delivered a major hurt to us or our marriage is not easy. This type of real forgiveness is vastly different from the peripheral forgiveness that we offer when we get in each other's way. Those simple times we say sorry almost out of habit rather than from the heart are not close to the depth of real forgiveness. Real forgiveness is much deeper. I am talking about times when we have really been hurt and somehow violated. Our natural emotion is to somehow save ourselves through revenge or retribution. We can justifiably feel superior. There is a guilty and innocent contrast. Our status as innocent victims gives us immense power over the guilty. This is where a commitment to stay made years ahead of the crisis is powerful. It gives us the platform to choose to stay rather than go as well as commitment to do the work needed to fix and forgive versus stagnate and punish. Forgiveness requires willingness to forgive.

Forgiveness means that we have to think about the other person. This is something that can be helped by a competent third party. A skilled counsellor or clergy can listen to your hurt but also listen with understanding to the one who did the hurting. When I have been in spots like that, the actions that happened often are not the absolute result of actions of the guilty party. There are circumstances that build toward actions that in themselves do not look that bad. However, as these things add up, they initiate something that in the end looks and is horribly wrong. The person who cheats may have been feeling isolated and alone for a long time before the infidelity happened. The person who made a damaging financial mistake may have been driven by intense pressure from the other to deliver the impossible. Part of this path to forgiveness is the realization that we are all imperfect human beings. There is often evidence that the man or woman who committed the offense was acting with a clouded sense of reality under the pressure of life. The person was trying to meet a need and that need may have been more than his or her immediate pleasure. Part of getting to the forgiveness point is an honest look at what the offending person did in the context of what was the person trying to do. What caused this person that we loved at one time to act in such a hurtful way? Is there any way to understand, at least a little bit, why they did what they did? Usually an honest look at the whole marriage will find some evidence of a deeper, more forgivable story beyond what we see at the peak of our anger. With that picture in hand, the choice to forgive gets easier and the path to repair much better.

Hard times will come to every marriage. We do not have a choice about that. What we do have a choice about is what happens afterward. The path to joy starts with being willing to choose forgiveness. That is critical to a heathy marriage. Yes, both people could stay in the marriage "for the children" or some other driver without forgiveness. But if forgiveness does not happen and one lives with a perpetual hammer of retribution over the other, joy will not be there for either.

We are imperfect human beings. In marriage, we discover that about ourselves and each other. Choosing to forgive is a powerful marriage builder. Like everything else in marriage, it takes two. But the joy possible from living without lasting bitterness and moving on to life after disaster is great. Jesus set the forgiveness bar high for us with his command to forgive beyond reason. In describing our obligation to forgive, Jesus said in Matthew 18:22, "I say to you, not seven times but seventy-seven times." Imagine how unbreakable a marriage would be if both spouses offer that level of forgiveness.

Chapter 12

PLAN RIGHT FROM THE START TO GROW OLD TOGETHER

In the title of this book, I offered to give you ten steps that will make your marriage unbreakable. Based on living these ten steps, I hope you see how a couple can have a marriage that is divorce proof and will last a lifetime. I hope also that you see how such a marriage will be joy filled. Now that you are at the end of this book, I hope you see how it is very possible for a woman and man to do this. Getting there takes a series of active choices. It takes two people united in life choices. One cannot, even with full personal commitment, do it alone. But when both enter and live marriage committed to these principles, they are set to live the dream of a lifelong, joy-filled marriage.

In summary, here are the ten steps:

1. Fully commit to a covenant marriage formed by free will commitment to lifelong fidelity and respect. In entering the covenant, both commit to never quit the marriage. Both commit to do the work necessary to make the marriage endure: repair what needs repairing and build for a lifetime together with no thought of exit.

2. Understand and appreciate the uniqueness of the history and traditions that come from the families of origin for husband and wife. Based on this foundation, both seek to reach a point where

      the "we" of the couple is special and prevails over their families of origin.

3. Make God a partner in the marriage with spirituality and prayer part of daily life. Pray together daily. Be an active part of a church or faith community.

4. Understand and appreciate the unique personalities of husband and wife. Building from that understanding, draw on strengths of both to make the couple greater than the sum of the parts.

5. Be unified and open in all financial matters with possession of material things in a proper and modest place, especially homes and cars. Include charity for others as a way of life.

6. Give to each other sexually, always using the gift of sex to unify and build the marriage. Seek always to please the other in ways that love the other as Christ loved his church.

7. Build a home that welcomes and nurtures children, always remembering that the best gift for a child is a strong marriage for the parents. Be unified in parenting, always choosing spouse and the marriage when choices need to be made.

8. Be open to new life by responsibly planning family size and timing of growth naturally.

9. Always practice the art of forgiveness and art of being forgiven.

10. Commit from the beginning to grow old together.

Depending on the source, research shows that couples who live this ten-point plan stand a 97 to 99 percent chance of living a lifelong first marriage. How can this be in a world where people talk about odds of survival of first marriages being only 50 percent? Think about the steps and what each means to marriage. First is the covenant commitment. That alone, if done in truth, is a guarantee of lifelong marriage. When both commit and back up the commitment to never quit with effort and action, divorce is never an option. Then there are the research-backed elements of praying together and natural family planning that are associated with nearly perfect marriage durability. Then add the presence of children that reduces the incidence of divorce. Then add unity in the two things that are the greatest causes of divorce: finance and sex. Unity in these things solidifies a couple and brings dreams fulfilled and joy to the marriage. Then add the appreciation for the unique gifts of background and personality that each brings to the marriage. This appreciation makes those differences blossom rather than be divisive. Finally, add the art of forgiveness and commitment to grow old together. All of these things add up to something wonderful. This all can be yours!

The final video segment we share with our marriage prep couples is a segment showing an older couple, probably in their eighties, preparing for bed. We witness very tender moments in their home, which once had children and busyness and is now quiet with just the two of them. We are told that his eyesight is failing. We see her apply eye drops to extend his vision. They quietly pray together in thanksgiving for the day in a way that shows thanksgiving for a lifetime of joy. I introduce the segment as one that "gets me every time." As a man who is much closer to the end of marriage than the beginning, I can see in that couple a future that will come quicker than I can imagine to Frances and me. Now if I live a normal life span, I have slightly over fifteen years left with forty-six years of marriage behind me. The game of life is now in the fourth quarter. At the end of the segment, the classroom is silent and still. I tell the group simply, "This is our wish for you."

Indeed, that is the wish for each of our couples and for you. The wish is that you will experience a full life together and realize the joy that is in lifelong marriage. I remember seeing my grandfather at the funeral of my grandmother. I grew up in a family that did not show emotion. Men did not cry, and there was no hugging or visible sign of affection. On that day of my grandmother's funeral, I saw my grandfather break down into uncontrollable tears. For years, that scene stayed with me and made me wonder if I would ever be capable of living that kind of love for someone. It was only after meeting Frances that that doubt went away. I started to discover what my grandfather had. I now know that on my wedding day, I had no idea how that kind of love really feels. Over the years, I have begun to know the feeling. It was probably around year forty that I really started to feel the deep emotion that comes from a full life together. There is nothing like it. When I hear of the "gray divorces," I compassionately think of the impossibility of rebuilding the kind of bond that comes from decades together. When I ponder the creation story of Genesis 2 and what Original Innocence was like, this lifelong marriage gives me a clue of what that was like. It is still here for us!

When I review the academic studies of lifelong marital happiness that show happiness at the end of a lifelong marriage equal to wedding day romance, I believe that to be possible and true. I feel it in my own marriage and see it in many others. While each couple that I know has had a unique walk through life, they all had the common commitment at the front end to marry for life. Though we did not have a clue what it would be like, we had the expectation that we would grow old together.

On your wedding day, or if you are married now, think back to your wedding day. Look at the one who is to become or is your partner in life *for* life. See the beauty. See the strength. See the dreams and hopes and all that is there. Freeze that image in your mind, and hold it for life. Pull it out when days are tough or you feel distance from your husband or wife. In the years to come, let that image remind you of all that was given to you on that day. Decades into marriage, you will look at your spouse with new eyes that will be rose colored from a life of love. You will see beauty and strength that no one else can see. You will feel joy that comes with appreciation for a gift that cannot be matched in this world. Once again, you will realize in human form how truly this person really meant "This is my body, mind, heart, and self all given to you." As we advance in age, we will slip in strength or beauty. But this will just add to the realization of how significant that gift to you was.

Commit at the beginning to grow old together. That was God's plan from the beginning. He saw it. It was then and is now very good. May the joy of a lifetime of love be yours in your unbreakable marriage. With God's blessings, amen!

About the Author

Jim Krupka brings a unique perspective as a clergyman, charity director, business executive, husband, and father. He has a passion for marriage. He has helped hundreds of couples prepare for and enrich their marriages and helped many people start anew after divorce. He has provided leadership and strategic guidance for charities at stages ranging from startup to mature. Professionally, he has more than thirty-five years of experience as a planner and executive for a *Fortune* 100 company as well as a regional entrepreneurial company. He and his wife of forty-six years have five grown children and operate a farm in northern Michigan.

Printed in the United States
by Baker & Taylor Publisher Services